DATA ANALYTICS FOR AUDITING USING ACL

4TH EDITION

Alvin A. Arens, Randal J. Elder, and Carol J. Borsum

Table of Contents

Introduction

The purpose of the Reference book is to help students learn ACL commands and other activities that are used in the assignments in the Instructions & Assignments book. The activities other than commands include only filters and computed fields. The use of the term *commands* in the remainder of the introduction implies both commands and other activities.

Quick Reference Guides

The Quick Reference Guides are integral parts of the Reference materials. There are two parts to the guide: one on the inside front cover of this book and the other on the inside back cover. The Quick Reference Guides include the following information:

- **Quick Reference Guide – Alphabetical (inside front cover).** This version of the Guide is useful if you know which command you will use and want to quickly find the command's Reference book page number.
- **Quick Reference Guide – Category of Command (inside back cover).** This version of the Guide is useful if you want brief information to decide the command to select. After deciding the command, you can also use it to locate the command's Reference book page number.

To help you identify command buttons, they are included on the top of both of the guides in alphabetical order with the command name immediately below the button.

Initial Use of the Reference Book

You will likely use the Reference book extensively when you are first learning the ACL commands, but rely on it less as you become more familiar with the software. Even users with considerable experience are likely to refer to the Reference book when they forget how to use certain commands. The Instructions & Assignments book will guide you in learning the commands in the Reference book. The commands are included in the Reference book in alphabetical order.

Suggested Way to Use the Reference Materials

The following are suggestions to help you effectively use the Reference book:

- While doing Chapters 3 through 5 of the Instructions & Assignments book, use the Reference book extensively to help you learn the uses of the commands as well as the steps to complete each command. The Reference book includes five parts for each command. You will learn ACL more effectively if you understand all five for each command, which will help you in later chapters as well as when you use it in business. The five parts are:

  - What the command is used for. **(Used For)**
  - When the command is likely to be used. **(When Used)**
  - Examples where the command used. **(Examples)**
  - The steps in using the command. **(Steps)**
  - The results of the command. **(Command Results)**

- In Chapters 3 through 5 of the Instructions & Assignments book, follow each of the Steps in the Reference book to make sure you understand what should be done to complete each command. Gaining a complete understanding of the steps in these three chapters will help you complete later chapters more effectively.

- In subsequent chapters use the **Quick Reference Guide – Category of Command** if you need guidance to help you identify a command button, decide the appropriate command, and/or locate the appropriate page in the Reference book if you need guidance to execute the command. Use the **Quick Reference Guide – Alphabetical** to help you identify the command button and/or locate the appropriate page in the Reference book if you know the appropriate command but need guidance to execute the command.

This page is intentionally blank.

Filters and Computed Fields

Filters
(Numeric, Character, and Date Fields)

Global Filters

Used For

To ask questions of data in a table without adding a new field.

When Used

Used extensively to ask a variety of questions before or after a command has been executed.

Examples

- Identify purchases over $5,000 in an accounts payable transaction table.
- Identify customers with a credit limit over $10,000 in an accounts receivable master file table.

Steps

You enter the expression builder either by clicking the Edit View Filter button ⓕ in an open table or clicking the If button while working with any ACL command. The illustrations in this section use the Edit view filter window, but the expression builder operates the same in an If window.

 📁 *Open the table you plan to build a filter for if it is not already open.*

 Click the Edit View Filter button ⓕ to open the Edit view filter window.

The Expression box is where you build filters using the available fields in the current table, as well as the operators (=, < >, AND, etc.). There are three components to a filter: (1) field, (2) operator and (3) a numeric value, character value, or date.

- *In the Available Fields portion of the window, double-click the name of the field for which you are building a filter. Notice that the field name is inserted in the Expression box.*
- *Use the operator buttons (=, +, <, >, etc.) and the numeric keypad on the keyboard to build the filter.*
- *Enter an appropriate string or value after the operator. Use the following guidelines:*

  - Enter numeric values as a number with no commas or dollar signs. For example, to enter $1,000, type 1000.
  - Enclose character values with one or two quotations. For example, to enter department D10, type "D10" or 'D10'. Be careful to use the same case as is used in the data field.
  - Click on the Date button located just below the mathematical operators to open the Date Selector box. Click the drop-down arrow to enter the monthly calendar box.

  - To select a month, click the right arrow to advance the month, or the left arrow to reverse the month.
  - To select the day, click the appropriate day in the calendar.
  - To select the year, click the year in the calendar and scroll to the appropriate year.
  - Click OK to add the date to the Expression box.

After you have completed the filter it should appear in the Expression box in the form at the top of the following page.

For more complex filters, use the AND, OR, or NOT operators and repeat the preceding process for each portion of the filter. After selecting an AND, OR or NOT, it is necessary to repeat all three components of the filter.

> ▪▫▪ *Click OK to complete the filter.*

The same table appears in view, but only the filtered records are included. An example follows.

> ▪▫▪ *If you want to change the filter, click ⓕⓧ again to return to the Edit View Filter window. Make changes in the filter and click OK.*

> ▪▫▪ *If you want to save the filtered data to a new table, use the Extract command. See page 44 for Extract command guidance. Save the table if you plan significant additional tests on the filtered data.*

You can also apply additional commands to a filtered table until you remove the filter.

> *Click the Remove Filter button ⊗ after you have completed all additional tests on the filtered table to return to the unfiltered table.*

Command Results

After a filter is applied to a table, only the records that meet the condition specified in the filter appear on the screen. The filtered data can be extracted into a new table or the filter can be removed to return to the original table.

Quick Filters

Quick filters are a subset of global filters. They are used to ask questions of data in an open table without using the Expression Builder. Quick filters are used extensively to ask a variety of questions when a record in the table can be used as a frame of reference. Examples of quick filters include:

- Identify all sales transactions for a specific customer in a sales transaction table.
- Identify all accounts receivable over an amount selected in a table of accounts receivable.

To create a quick filter, complete the following steps.

> 📁 *Open a table in which you want to apply the quick filter* (typically a table is already open when you use a quick filter). A table appears, similar to the one that follows.

	Product_Number	Product_Class	Location	Product_Description	Product_Status	Unit_Cost	Cost_Date	Sales_Price
1	070104347	07	06	LATEX SEMI-GLOSS ORANGE	A	6.87	10/10/2018	9.99
2	070104397	07	06	LATEX SEMI-GLOSS CARAMEL	A	6.87	10/10/2018	9.99
3	070104177	07	06	LATEX SEMI-GLOSS LILAC	A	-6.87	10/10/2018	9.99
4	070104677	07	06	LATEX SEMI-GLOSS APRICOT	A	6.87	10/10/2018	9.99
5	070104657	07	06	LATEX SEMI-GLOSS PINK	A	6.87	10/10/2018	9.99
6	070104327	07	06	LATEX SEMI-GLOSS YELLOW	A	6.87	10/10/2018	9.99
7	070104377	07	06	LATEX SEMI-GLOSS GREEN	A	6.87	10/10/2018	9.99
8	030414313	03	03	METRIC TOOL SET 3/8" DR	A	47.00	09/30/2018	59.98
9	030414283	03	03	METRIC SOCKET SET 11 PC	A	18.00	09/30/2018	25.98
10	030412553	03	03	6 PC OPEN END WRENCH SET	A	11.53	09/30/2018	15.98
11	030412753	03	03	6 PC BOX END WRENCH SET	A	12.50	09/30/2018	18.49
12	030412903	03	03	8 PC METRIC HEX KEYS	A	2.48	09/30/2018	3.49
13	034255003	03	03	PARKER PROPANE KIT (7PC)	U	8.40	03/30/2018	14.98
14	030364163	03	03	TAP & DIE SET 41 PIECES	A	49.60	03/30/2018	69.98
15	030321663	03	03	SCREW DRIVER 1/8 X 4 SL	A	0.73	03/30/2018	1.69
16	030321683	03	03	SCREW DRIVER 1/4 X 6 SL	A	1.47	03/30/2018	2.59
17	030322303	03	03	SCREW DRIVER NO.3 PHILL	A	1.22	03/30/2018	2.29
18	030324803	03	03	ARC JOINT PLIERS 6"	A	3.99	03/30/2018	4.69
19	030324883	03	03	ARC JOINT PLIERS 16"	A	9.40	03/30/2018	14.98
20	030030323	03	03	LONG NOSE PLIERS 7"	A	5.00	05/10/2018	6.98
21	030934423	03	04	DIAGONAL CUTTING PLIERS	A	4.98	05/10/2018	7.79
22	030303413	03	03	8 OZ BALL PEIN HAMMER	A	3.90	08/10/2018	4.69
23	030303403	03	03	12 OZ BALL PEIN HAMMER	A	4.12	08/10/2018	5.29
24	030303343	03	03	STRAIGHT CLAW HAMMER	A	8.83	08/10/2018	12.98
25	130305603	13	03	#4 SMOOTH PLANE	A	14.12	10/12/2018	22.98
26	030309373	03	03	HEAVY DUTY BRACE	A	10.12	10/12/2018	16.98
27	030302903	03	03	4 PC CHISEL SET	A	10.12	10/12/2018	16.98
28	030302303	03	03	MITRE BOX 21"	A	41.23	10/12/2018	54.95
29	093788411	09	04	1" GARDEN HOSE	A	1.40	09/30/2018	3.98
30	090506331	09	04	5 PIECE GARDEN TOOL SET	A	-6.80	08/10/2018	10.98
31	090501541	09	04	24" LEAF RAKE	A	3.00	08/10/2018	5.99
32	090501551	09	04	20" LEAF RAKE	A	1.83	08/10/2018	2.99
33	090501051	09	04	11" SPADING FORK	A	4.82	08/10/2018	9.99
34	090504061	09	04	54" EDGING TURF	A	1.37	08/10/2018	2.49

 Left-click then right-click the cell in the table that you want to apply the filter.

From the shortcut menu, choose Quick Filter, then left-click on the logical operator you want to choose for your filter. The logical operator options are below:

Date field operators	Numeric and Character field operators
On	Equal
Not On	Not Equal
After	Greater Than
On or After	Greater Than or Equal To
Before	Less Than
On or Before	Less Than or Equal To

Command Results

The results will be the same as a filter that has been built with the Expression Builder. An example follows.

	Product_Number	Product_Class	Location	Product_Description	Product_Status	Unit_Cost
8	030414313	03	03	METRIC TOOL SET 3/8" DR	A	47.00
14	030364163	03	03	TAP & DIE SET 41 PIECES	A	49.60
28	030302303	03	03	MITRE BOX 21"	A	41.23
43	090584072	09	04	22" SELF-PROPELLED MOW	A	173.80
44	090585322	09	04	18" REEL MOWER	A	137.80
48	090081001	09	04	SUPER CALLUM LEAF MULCH	A	155.80
70	052720305	05	05	1X8 SHIPLAP PER MFBM	A	41.00
71	052720615	05	05	2X4 RANDOM PER MFBM	A	41.00
97	080935428	08	02	DUAL LEVER FAUCET -SPRAY	A	44.24
98	080435438	08	02	DUAL LEVER FAUCET-NO-SPR	A	40.24
134	060217066	06	02	ALUMINUM DOOR	A	87.40
136	040220074	04	03	3/8" COMPACT DRILL PRESS	A	62.00
140	040243224	04	03	2 SP ROTARY SANDER	A	52.80
141	040232194	04	03	12 SP AUTO SCROLLER SAW	A	59.60
152	040270324	04	03	RADIAL ARM SAW 10" HD	A	381.20

< < End of File > >

You can extract or save the information in the same way as for a filter. You can also go directly to the filter in the Expression Builder by clicking on the Edit View Filter button ⓕˣ, or you can return to the unfiltered table by clicking the Remove Filter button ⊗.

Finally, a quick filter can be applied to table data that has already been filtered. To add a quick filter to an existing filtered table, do the following:

- *Left-click then right-click a cell in the table.*
- *From the shortcut menu, choose Quick Filter, then click on the operator AND or OR.*
- *Left-click on the logical operator you want to choose for your quick filter.*

Command Filters

Used For

To filter data within an ACL command to restrict which records in a table are analyzed with the command.

When Used

Used extensively to apply ACL commands to certain records in a table.

Examples

- Determine the total customer balances outstanding greater than 90 days.
- Determine the average gross pay of employees in a specific work department.

Steps

You first initiate the ACL command that you want to run on certain items in an ACL table. You then use a command filter to restrict the application of the chosen command to records that meet the filter criteria.

- *Open the table you plan to build a command filter for if it is not already open.*
- *Start the process of running an ACL command, such as the Count, Total, or Sort command.*
- *Select the field(s) on which you want to run the ACL command.*
- *Click the If button to open an Expression Builder window for the chosen ACL command. An example of the Expression Builder window for the Sort command follows.*

Expression Builder - Sort: If

Expression

Verify

Save As

Available Fields

Name	Title	Start
NO1	NO1	1
NAME	NAME	12
ADDRESS	ADDRESS	44
CITY	CITY	76
STATE	STATE	97
ZIP	ZIP	99
LIMIT	LIMIT	104
SALES_...	SALES_REP_NO	112

Operators: = <> And + - < > Or * / <= >= Not ^ ()

Date & Time...

Filters

Variables

OUTPUTFOLDER
TOTAL1
WRITE1

Functions

All

ABS(number)
AGE(date/datetime/string <,cutoff_date>)
ALLTRIM(string)
ASCII(character)
AT(occurence_num , search_for_string , withi
BETWEEN(value , min , max)
BIT(byte_location)
BLANKS(count)
BYTE(byte_location)
CDOW(date/datetime , length)
CHR(number)
CLEAN(string <,extra_invalid_characters>)
CMOY(date/datetime , length)
COS(radians)
CTOD(string/number <,format>)
CTODT(string/number <,format>)
CTOT(string/number)

☑ Paste Parameters

From Table

Customer

OK   Cancel   Help

- *In the Available Fields portion of the dialog box, double-click on the name of the field for which you are building a filter.*
- *Use the operator buttons (=, +, <, >, etc.) and the numeric keypad on the keyboard to build the filter.*
- *Enter the appropriate string or value after the operator, using the same guidelines described on page 6 in the Global Filters section.*

After you have completed the expression, it should appear in the Expression box in a format similar to the following. Note that this illustration is for the Sort command and your window will look different if you are starting with a different ACL command (Total, Count, Statistics, for example).

- Click OK to complete the filter and return to the ACL command window.
- *Complete the steps for the ACL command you are preforming.* The command will now be performed on the filtered data, using the condition(s) in the command filter you created.

Computed Fields
(Numeric, Character, and Date Fields)

Used For

To ask questions of data in a table by adding a new field. The new field is typically derived from calculations on other fields in the table, usually numeric fields.

When Used

When the auditor wants to perform calculations based on information in a table. The auditor can add a computed field to a table view even though it is not included in the client's data file.

Examples

- Add a field of recalculated net pay in a payroll transaction file table based on gross pay and withheld amounts. Compare the computed field with the net pay field in the table to isolate differences.
- Add a field of recalculated inventory value at cost to a year-end inventory table based on units on hand and cost per unit. Compare the computed field with the existing total cost field.

Steps

- *Open a table in which you want to add a computed field.*
- *Click Edit → Table Layout.* The following window appears.

		Table Layout Options	Edit Fields/Expressions	Add a New Data Filter			

All fields

Name	Title	Start	Category	Length	Decimals
WORK_DEPT_	WORK_DEPT_	7	C	3	0
TAXABLE_AMOUNT	TAXABLE_AM...	22	N	11	2
PAY_DATE	PAY_DATE	45	D	10	0
NET_PAY	NET_PAY	33	N	12	2
GROSS_PAY	GROSS_PAY	10	N	12	2
EMPLOYEE_NUMBER	EMPLOYEE_N...	1	C	6	0
CHECK_NUMBER	CHECK_NUMB...	55	C	8	0

```
ASCII    ....|....10...|....20...|....30...|....40...|....50...|....60.. ▲
  1    000010A00    4395.83    879.17    3516.6609/15/201812346
  2    000020B01    3437.50    687.50    2750.0009/15/201812347
  3    000030C01    3187.50    637.50    2550.0009/15/201812348
  4    000050E01    3347.92    669.58    2678.3409/15/201812349
  5    000060D11    2687.50    537.50    2150.0009/15/201812350
  6    000070D21    3014.17    602.83    2411.3409/15/201812351
  7    000100E21    2179.17    435.83    1743.3409/15/201812352
```

Click the Add a New Expression button 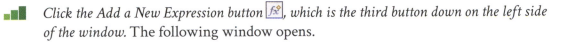, which is the third button down on the left side of the window. The following window opens.

Add a name for the computed field in the Name box. Also add a column title in the *Alternative Column Title box.* Use names for both that are consistent in style with those already in the Table Layout. When you add the computed field to a table view in the future, the name in the Alternative Column Title box is included in the table.

Click the Expression button 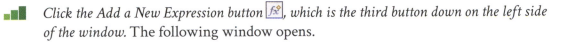, which is located to the right of the Name box. The following Expression window appears.

The Expression box is where you build expressions using the available fields in the dialog box, as well as the operators (=, <>, AND, etc.). There are three components to an expression: (1) field, (2) operator and (3) a numeric value, character value, or date.

- *In the Available Fields portion of the dialog box, double-click the name of the field for which you are building an expression.* Notice that the field name is inserted in the Expression box.

- *Use the operator buttons (=, +, <, >, etc.) and the numeric keypad on the keyboard to build the expression.*

- *Enter an appropriate string or value after the operator.* Use the following guidelines:

  - Enter numeric values as a number with no commas or dollar signs. For example, to enter $1,000, type 1000.

  - Enclose character values with one or two quotations. For example, to enter department D10, type "D10" or 'D10'. Be careful to use the same case as is used in the data field.

  - Click on the Date button located just below the mathematical operators to open the Date Selector box. Click the drop-down arrow to enter the monthly calendar box.

Date & Time Selector			X
☑ Select Date		☐ Select Time	
Thursday , February 09, 2017 ▾		2:42:35 PM	↕
OK	Cancel	Help	

  - To select a month, click the right arrow to advance the month, or the left arrow to reverse the month.

  - To select the day, click the appropriate day in the calendar.

  - To select the year, click the year in the calendar and scroll to the appropriate year.

  - Click OK to add the date to the Expression box.

After you have completed the expression it should appear in the Expression box in the form illustrated at the top of the following page.

For more complex expressions, use the AND, OR, or NOT operators and repeat the preceding process for each portion of the expression. After selecting an AND, OR or NOT, it is necessary to repeat all three components of the expression.

> *After building the expression, click OK to return to the previous window.* Following is an example of a completed window for a computed field.

> *Click the Accept Entry button* ✔ *to save the new computed field.*

Command Result

The new computed field is added to the list of other fields in the Table Layout window but it has not been added to the table view. See RecalcNetPay in the Table Layout window below.

The new field can be added to the table view by completing the following steps.

- Close the Edit Fields/Expressions window if it is still open.

- Right-click the column heading to the right of where you want the new computed field to appear in the table view. Note: Be sure to click the column heading and not just a cell in the table. If you do this correctly, the entire column is highlighted.

- Click Add Columns from the drop-down menu.

- Double-click on the name of the new computed field you just created.

- Click OK. The new computed field should now appear in the table view.

- If you wish to move the new column, left-click and hold the column heading and drag it to the desired location.

Note: You do not need to add the new computed field to the view to run commands on that field.

Commands — Alphabetical

COMMAND

Age Command
(Date Fields)

Used For

To aggregate or accumulate data in a table by age, using intervals from a specified cutoff date. Aging can be done for all records in a table or for records that meet a specified condition.

When Used

Whenever the auditor wants numeric information about the age of items in a table. The auditor can specify the aging intervals and often ages the same table using different intervals until the values in each category correspond to the auditor's needs.

Examples

- Age year-end accounts receivable into 30 days or less, 31–60 days, etc.
- Age year-end accounts receivable for one customer.
- Age year-end accounts receivable for each district.

TASK #1 — Age All Records in a Table Using a Specified Cutoff Date

Steps

 Click Analyze → Age to open the Age command dialog. Each date field in the table is listed in the Age On drop-down list box.

- Use the Age On drop-down arrow to select the date field you want to run the Age command on.

- In the Subtotal Fields portion of the command dialog, click on the name(s) of the numeric field(s) you want to list for each aging interval. Use the Shift or Control key to select multiple fields. Note: Holding the Shift key selects multiple fields in order, while holding the Control key selects multiple fields that are not in order.

- Enter a date in the Cutoff Date box using the calendar. This date is used to calculate the aging. It is typically the client's year-end date.

ACL uses the following default interval points for aging: 0, 30, 60, 90, 120, and 10,000 days. The last interval point — 10,000 — is helpful for isolating unusually old items. These interval points will produce the following aging periods: 0–29 days, 30–59 days, 60–89 days, 90–119 days, and 120–10,000 days.

- If you want to change the aging period interval points, type new amounts in the Aging Periods box.

A completed Age command dialog with changed interval points of 0, 30, 60, 120 is shown below.

- If you want to suppress items outside of the specified aging periods, click the More tab and click the Suppress Others radio button.

- Click OK to run the Age command.

Command Results

The command results show each aging category, the number of records in each category, the total value for the numeric field(s) accumulated in each category, and percentage information. An example of Age command results follows.

As of:	04/26/2017 12:46:53
Command:	AGE ON Invoice_Date CUTOFF 20180413 INTERVAL 0,30,60,120 TO SCREEN
Table:	Trans

Minimum encountered was -262
Maximum encountered was 101

Days	Count	Percent of Count
≤0	246	72.57%
0 - 29	29	8.55%
30 - 59	33	9.73%
60 - 120	31	9.14%
Totals	**339**	**100%**

TASK #2 — Age All Records in a Table that Meet a Certain Condition Using a Specified Cutoff Date (If box)

The age command can also be used with a filter to age certain records. An example is to run a conditional command to age all transaction amounts for a specific district. Do the following to run a conditional Age command:

Steps

- *Complete all steps in Task #1, except do not Click OK to run the command.*
- *Click the If button.*
- *Build the filter in the Expression box. See pages 6 through 9 for guidance on using the Expression box.*

Expression Builder - Age: If

Expression

Invoice_Amount > 5000

Verify

Save As

Available Fields

Name	Title	Start
Quantity	Quantity	20
Product_Number	Product_Num...	9
Product_Class	Product_Class	18
Invoice_Number	Invoice_Number	1
Invoice_Date	Invoice_Date	46
Invoice_Amount	Invoice_Amount	28

Functions

All

ABS(number)
AGE(date/datetime/string <,cutoff_date>)
ALLTRIM(string)
ASCII(character)
AT(occurence_num , search_for_string , withi
BETWEEN(value , min , max)
BIT(byte_location)
BLANKS(count)
BYTE(byte_location)
CDOW(date/datetime , length)
CHR(number)
CLEAN(string <,extra_invalid_characters>)
CMOY(date/datetime , length)
COS(radians)
CTOD(string/number <,format>)
CTODT(string/number <,format>)
CTOT(string/number)

Filters

Variables

OUTPUTFOLDER

From Table

Trans

☑ Paste Parameters

OK   Cancel   Help

Click OK to run the command with an If condition.

Command Results

The command results show the following for the records selected in the filter: each aging category, the number of records in each category, the total value for the numeric field(s) accumulated in each category, and percentage information.

As of: 02/14/2017 14:02:14

Command: AGE ON Invoice_Date CUTOFF 20180413 INTERVAL 0,30,60,90,120,10000 IF Invoice_Amount > 5000 TO SCREEN

Table: Trans

Condition: Invoice_Amount > 5000 (17 records matched)

Minimum encountered was -244
Maximum encountered was 97

Days	Count	Percent of Count
<0	12	70.59%
0 - 29	0	0%
30 - 59	3	17.65%
60 - 89	1	5.88%
90 - 119	1	5.88%
120 - 10,000	0	0%
Totals	**17**	**100%**

TASK #3 — Age All Records in a Table by a Character Field

The age command can also be used with a filter to age certain records by classification. An example is to run a conditional command to age all transaction amounts in each of several districts. Do the following to run a conditional Age command for each unique item in a character field.

Steps

 Before aging records in a table by a character field, you must first sort the table, by the character you select, into a new table. See page 81 for the Sort Command. You will then do the aging on the new table.

 Complete all steps in Task #1 for Age, except do not Click OK to run the command.

 Click the More tab to open the More window.

Age				
Main	More	Output		

Scope
- ◉ All
- ○ First
- ○ Next

While...

☐ Suppress Others

Break...

☐ Append To Existing File

OK   Cancel   Help

 Click on the Break button to access the Selected Fields window.

 Select the character field you want to classify by and make sure it is included in the Selected Fields box.

 Click OK to return to the Main command dialog.

 Click OK to run the Age command, organized by a character field.

Command Results

The command results show a separate aging for each unique item in the character field you selected.

As of: 02/14/2017 14:25:36

Command: AGE ON Invoice_Date CUTOFF 20180413 INTERVAL 0,30,60,90,120,10000 TO SCREEN KEY Product_Number

Table: Inventory_Sort_By_ProdNum

Product_Number: 010102710

Days	Count	Percent of Count
≤0	1	50%
0 - 29	0	0%
30 - 59	0	0%
60 - 89	1	50%
90 - 119	0	0%
120 - 10,000	0	0%
Totals	2	100%

Product_Number: 010102840

Days	Count	Percent of Count
≤0	2	66.67%
0 - 29	0	0%
30 - 59	1	33.33%
60 - 89	0	0%
90 - 119	0	0%
120 - 10,000	0	0%
Totals	3	100%

Classify Command
(Character Fields)

Used For

To count and aggregate the number and percentage of records related to each unique value of a character field and to subtotal specified numeric fields for each of these unique values.

When Used

When the auditor wants to obtain information about each unique character in a field, often to evaluate the possibility of unusual subtotals. Frequently used as an analytical procedure on every character field with three or fewer characters.

Classify, Summarize, and Cross-tabulate are all ways of accumulating information. The decision as to which one to use depends on the following:

- To accumulate percentages, use Classify.
- If data needs to be organized by a date field, use Summarize.
- If data needs to be organized by more than one character field simultaneously (e.g. by product number, by location), use Summarize or Cross-tabulate, depending on personal preference.

Examples

- Determine which sales territory in a sales data file had the most revenue for a fiscal year.
- Determine which department in a payroll transaction file has the highest average gross pay per pay period.

Steps

Click Analyze → Classify to open the Classify command dialog. Each character field in the table is listed in the Classify On drop-down list box. (See the top of the following page.)

- *Use the Classify On drop-down arrow to select the character field you want to run the Classify command on.*

- *In the Subtotal Fields portion of the command dialog, click on the name(s) of the numeric field(s) you want to list for each classification. Use the Shift or Control key to select multiple fields.*

By default, ACL sends the results of the Classify command to the screen. ACL can also send these results to an ACL table, where they can be further analyzed. To send the results to the screen:

- *Click OK to send the results to the screen.*

To send the results to an ACL table for further analysis, do the following:

- *Click the Output tab.*
- *Click the File radio button.*
- *Type a table name in the Name box. Note: It is helpful to enter a meaningful name, such as Sales_By_Prod_Class. A completed example is shown at the top of the following page.*

Classify

Main | More | **Output**

To
- ○ Screen
- ○ Graph
- ○ Print
- ● File

As

File Type: [ACL Table ▾]

[Name...] [WORKDEPTSUBTOTALGROSS]

☐ Local

Optional

[Header...] [_____]

[Footer...] [_____]

[OK] [Cancel] [Help]

 Click OK to send the results to an ACL table.

If the results are sent to an ACL table, the default view shows the classified table.

Command Results

The command results show the following for each classification:

- The number of records in each classification.
- The percentage of records in the classification.
- The total of the numeric field(s) selected in the Subtotal Fields box for the classification.
- For the first numeric field selected in the Subtotal Fields box, ACL shows the accumulated classification amount as a percentage of the total amount.

An example of command results for a Classify command follows:

As of: 02/14/2017 14:41:11
Command: CLASSIFY ON WORK_DEPT_ SUBTOTAL GROSS_PAY TO SCREEN
Table: Payroll

WORK_DEPT_	Count	Percent of Count	Percent of Field	GROSS_PAY
«3 spaces»	1	2.22%	0%	0.00
A00	5	11.11%	17.09%	17,020.83
B01	1	2.22%	3.45%	3,437.50
C01	4	8.89%	9.95%	9,907.49
D11	11	24.44%	23.15%	23,051.69
D21	7	15.56%	15.04%	14,973.34
E01	1	2.22%	3.36%	3,347.92
E11	6	13.33%	9.82%	9,782.50
E21	8	17.78%	16.47%	16,401.69
E83	1	2.22%	1.67%	1,662.50
Totals	**45**	**100%**	**100%**	**99,585.46**

Count Command

Used For

To count records in an entire table or to count records in a table that meet a certain condition.

When Used

Should be used for every table when the table is first established. The ACL record count should be compared to information received from the IT department.

Examples

- Count the number of records in a table of sales invoices.
- Count the number of records for sales district #4 in a table of sales invoices.

TASK # 1 — Count the Number of Records in a Table

The Count command should only be used for a table with no filter when it is important to have the count documented in the Log. If no record count is needed in the Log, determine the record count from the bottom of the open table. In the table below the record count is 44.

Steps When a Record Count is Needed in the Log

Click Analyze → Count to open the Count command dialog.

Count

| Main | More |

If...

OK   Cancel   Help

Click OK to run the Count Command.

Unlike all other ACL commands, the results of this type of Count command (Task #1) do not automatically appear on the right portion of the screen. To view the command results, complete the following steps:

Click the Log tab in the lower-left corner of the main window. Information similar to the following should appear in the Project Navigator section of the main window.

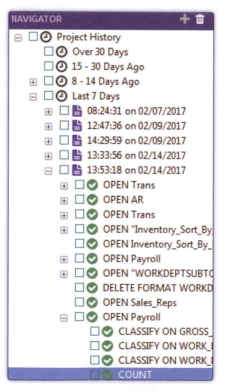

NAVIGATOR

Project History
Over 30 Days
15 - 30 Days Ago
8 - 14 Days Ago
Last 7 Days
08:24:31 on 02/07/2017
12:47:36 on 02/09/2017
14:29:59 on 02/09/2017
13:33:56 on 02/14/2017
13:53:18 on 02/14/2017
OPEN Trans
OPEN AR
OPEN Trans
OPEN "Inventory_Sort_By
OPEN Inventory_Sort_By_
OPEN Payroll
OPEN "WORKDEPTSUBTC
DELETE FORMAT WORKD
OPEN Sales_Reps
OPEN Payroll
CLASSIFY ON GROSS_
CLASSIFY ON WORK_
CLASSIFY ON WORK_
COUNT

Double-click on the last item, which says "COUNT."

Command Results

The command results in the right portion of the main window show the number of records in the table. This result should be compared to documentation received from the IT department or to an external source such as a printed report to assure completeness of the table.

As of:	02/14/2017 15:06:09
Command:	COUNT
Table:	Payroll

45 records counted

TASK # 2 — Count the Number of Records in a Table that Meet a Certain Condition

The Count command is most often used in a table where the auditor has used a filter to create a new table and wants a record count of the records meeting the condition specified in the filter. The Count command is illustrated after a filter is applied.

Steps

After a filter is applied to a table, observe that there is now a ?/ in the lower-left corner that replaces the original count. For the table below it is ?/152.

    Click Analyze → Count Records to open the Count command dialog.

    Click OK.

Command Results

The record count is shown on the bottom of the window replacing the ?. See the table that follows. The 7/152 means that 7 is the count of the filtered table of the total record count of 152.

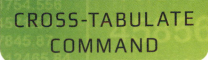

Cross-tabulate Command
(Character Fields)

Used For

To count and aggregate records simultaneously using two character fields and a related numeric field. Cross-tabulate is similar to Summarize, but the results appear in a convenient row/column grid form.

When Used

When the auditor wants to obtain information about two character fields simultaneously, often to evaluate the possibility of unusual subtotals. Frequently used as an analytical procedure.

Summarize and Cross-tabulate are both ways of accumulating information on two fields simultaneously. The decision as to which one to use depends on the following:

- If one of the fields is a date field, use Summarize.
- If both fields are character fields, use Summarize or Cross-tabulate, depending on personal preference. Cross-tabulate results are shown in row/column format; Summarize results are not.

Examples

- Accumulate sales volume per salesperson in each territory from information in the sales transaction file.
- Determine quantity on hand by location and product class for an inventory data file.

Steps

Click Analyze → Cross-tab to open the Cross-tabulate command dialog. (See the top of the following page.)

The cross-tabulate command allows you to accumulate numeric data in rows and columns using a combination of two character fields. After you decide which two character fields to use for the command, it is helpful to choose the character field with the most unique entries as your selection in the Rows drop-down box.

> *Select one character field in the Rows box by clicking once on the field name.*

Next, select the character field for the Columns box.

> *Click the drop-down arrow beneath the Columns button to view all available character fields.*

> *Select one character field in the Columns box by clicking once on the field name.*

Next, in the Subtotal Fields box, select the numeric field(s) that you want to have totaled for each cell in the Cross-tabulate grid.

> *Click on the name of the numeric field(s) in the Subtotal Fields box to be totaled. Use the Shift or Control key to select more than one field.*

In addition to accumulating numeric totals for each cell in a cross-tabulate grid, you can also request a record count for each cell. This is important if you need to know how many records are included in the numeric total for each unique combination of the two selected character fields.

If you want to include a record count for each cell in the cross-tabulate grid, click the Include Count checkbox.

Next, select the form of output for the cross-tabulate results.

Click the Output tab.

By default, ACL sends the results of the Cross-tabulate command to an ACL table unless you have already sent a Cross-tabulate command result to the screen or printer during the same ACL session.

- *To send the results to the screen, select the Screen radio button if not already selected.*
- *To send the results to a printer, select the Print radio button if not already selected. Then select Print in the Print window.*
- *To send the results to an ACL table, make sure the File radio button is selected and type a table name in the Name box.* Note: It is helpful to enter a meaningful name, such as Purchases_CROSSTAB_ItemNo_Loc.
- *Click OK.*

If the Cross-tabulate command results are saved to a File, the command creates a new table that contains the cross-tabulated data. The new table will be the one in the View window.

Command Results

An example of command results for a Cross-tabulate command printed to the screen follows:

As of: 02/14/2017 15:50:43
Command: CROSSTAB ON Product_Class COLUMNS Product_Class SUBTOTAL Quantity_On_Hand TO SCREEN
Table: Inventory

Product_Class	Quantity_On_Hand Product Class 01	Quantity_On_Hand Product Class 02	Quantity_On_Hand Product Class 03	Quantity_On_Hand Product Class 04	Quantity_On_Hand Product Class 05	Quantity_On_Hand Product Class 06
01	2,634	0	0	0	0	0
02	0	3,087	0	0	0	0
03	0	0	12,531	0	0	0
04	0	0	0	4,760	0	0
05	0	0	0	0	89,466	0
06	0	0	0	0	0	2,915
07	0	0	0	0	0	0
08	0	0	0	0	0	0
09	0	0	0	0	0	0
13	0	0	0	0	0	0
18	0	0	0	0	0	0
Totals	2,634	3,087	12,531	4,760	89,466	2,915

Duplicates Command
(Numeric, Character, and Date Fields)

Used For

To check for duplicate records with the same values, typically document or record numbers.

When Used

Whenever the auditor is concerned that there are duplicates in a sequence of numbers, usually document numbers.

Examples

- Detect duplicate check numbers in a check register table.
- Detect duplicate vendor numbers in a vendor master file table.

Steps

▬ *Click Analyze → Duplicates to open the Duplicates command dialog.* Each field in the table is listed in the Duplicates command dialog.

▬ *In the Duplicates On portion of the command dialog, click on the name of the field(s) on which you want to run the Duplicates command. Use the Shift or Control key to select multiple fields.*

You may wish to generate other information for any duplicate records. Using the preceding table as an example, it might be helpful to know the pay date, employee number, and gross pay for any duplicate check numbers. The List Fields portion of the Duplicates command dialog shows the available fields that can be listed for any duplicates.

 In the List Fields portion of the command dialog, click on the name of the field(s) you want to list for each duplicate. Use the Shift or Control key to select multiple fields.

By default, the results of the Duplicates test are sent to a file unless you have already sent a Duplicates command result to the screen or printer during the same ACL session. Usually, screen output suffices. To change the output location to screen, do the following:

 Click the Output tab.

 Click the Screen radio button if not already selected.

 Click OK to complete the Duplicates command.

Command Results

This command will display the record number and key field if no fields are selected from the List Fields box. If fields are selected from the List Fields box, as in the example, the command output will display the key field and all of the fields selected in the List Fields box, but not the record number. Following is an illustration of Duplicates command results where an item was selected in the List Fields box.

As of:	02/16/2017 10:58:18
Command:	DUPLICATES ON EMPLOYEE_NUMBER OTHER EMPLOYEE_NUMBER CHECK_NUMBER GROSS_PAY PAY_DATE PRESORT TO SCREEN
Table:	Payroll

1 duplicates detected

Duplicates:

EMPLOYEE_NUMBER	CHECK_NUMBER	GROSS_PAY	PAY_DATE
000320	12376	1,662.50	09/15/2018
000320	12377	1,662.50	09/15/2018

Export Command

(Numeric, Character, and Date Fields)

Used For

To export data from an existing ACL table into a file that can be used by other software packages for further processing. ACL can export data into the following formats:

- Microsoft Excel 2.1 (.xls), 97-2003 (.xls), and 07-2010 (.xlsx)
- Text (.txt)
- Delimited text (.del)
- Microsoft Access (.mdb)
- Windows clipboard for pasting into other documents or applications
- XML (.xml)
- JSON (.json)
- dBASE III PLUS (.dbf)
- ACL GRC (export exceptions to the Results Manager module of ACL GRC)

Instructions for two of these file formats are included in this section: Text and Microsoft Excel.

When Used

When the auditor believes certain tasks can be performed on a table more conveniently in an alternative file format or when the data in the table is to be used by client personnel and they prefer the information in an alternative file format.

Examples

- Create a Text file to be used for accounts receivable confirmation by extracting information from the year-end accounts receivable and customer master file tables.
- Export sales price and cost data to Microsoft Excel from an inventory transaction table for further analysis.

TASK # 1 — Export Data to a Text File

Steps

- ▪▮▮ 🔲 *Click Data → Export to Other Application to open the Export dialog box.*
- ▪▮▮ *Select Text (*.txt) in the Export As drop-down list box. See below for the command dialog illustration.*

Export						
Main	**More**					

Name	Title	Start	Category	Length	D
ADDRESS	ADDRESS	44	C	32	0
CITY	CITY	76	C	21	0
LIMIT	LIMIT	104	N	8	0
NAME	NAME	12	C	32	0
NO1	NO1	1	C	11	0
SALES_REP_NO	SALES_REP_NO	112	C	5	0
STATE	STATE	97	C	2	0
ZIP	ZIP	99	C	5	0

Export Fields...

◉ Fields   ○ View

Export As
Text (*.txt) ▼

Export Options
☐ Export with field names

If...

To...   Customer_Mail_List

OK   Cancel   Help

- ▪▮▮ *In the Export Fields portion of the command dialog, click on the name of the field(s) you want to include in the mail merge file. Use the Shift or Control key to select multiple fields.*
- ▪▮▮ *If you want only certain records to be included in the mail merge (for example, all customers with amounts due for more than 120 days), click the If button, build a filter, and then click OK to return to the main Export command dialog. Otherwise, skip this step.*
- ▪▮▮ *Type a descriptive file name in the To box. Do not add the .txt file extension; ACL does this automatically.*
- ▪▮▮ *Click OK to run the command.*

Command Results

The command results show the name and location of the exported Text file, as well as a list of fields that were exported from the original table. The exported Text file is now ready to be imported into MS Word or other software. Although you cannot see the file in the Overview section of the window, you can locate the file using Windows Explorer and the file location described in the command results portion of the window. See the top of the following page for an example of Export command results for a Text file.

> **Command:** EXPORT FIELDS NO1 NAME ADDRESS ASCII TO "Customer_Mail_List"
>
> ```
> 09:48:51 - 04/28/2017
> 64 records produced
> Output to C:\Users\Carol\Documents\ACL Data\Sample Data Files\Customer_Mail_List.txt is done
> ```

TASK # 2 — Export Data to Microsoft Excel

Steps

 Click Data → Export to Other Application to open the Export command dialog.

Select Excel in the Export As drop-down list box.

Name	Title	Start	Category	Len
ZIP	ZIP	99	C	5
STATE	STATE	97	C	2
SALES_REP_NO	SALES_REP_NO	112	C	5
NO1	NO1	1	C	11
NAME	NAME	12	C	32
LIMIT	LIMIT	104	N	8
CITY	CITY	76	C	21
ADDRESS	ADDRESS	44	C	32

Export Fields...

Fields / View

Export As: Excel (*.xlsx)

Export Options
Add worksheet
Customer

If...
To...   Cust_Credit_Limit

OK   Cancel   Help

In the Export Fields portion of the command dialog, click on the name of the field(s) you want to include in the Excel file. Use the Shift or Control key to select multiple fields.

If you want only certain records to be included in the Excel file, click the If button, build a filter, and then click OK to return to the main Export command dialog. Otherwise, skip this step.

Type a descriptive file name in the To box. Do not add the .xlsx file extension; ACL does this automatically.

Click OK to run the command.

Command Results

The command results show the name and location of the exported Excel file, as well as a list of fields that were exported from the original table. The exported file is now ready to be imported in Excel. Although you cannot see the file in the Overview section of the window, you can locate the file using Windows Explorer and the file location described in the command results portion of the window. An example of Export command results for an Excel file follows:

```
Command:  EXPORT FIELDS NO1 NAME XLSX TO "Cust_Credit_Limit" WORKSHEET Customer


11:16:37 - 02/16/2017
64 records produced
Output to C:\Users\Jennifer\Documents\ACL Data\Sample Data Files\Cust_Credit_Limit.xlsx is done
```

Extract Command

(Numeric, Character, and Date Fields)

Used For

To isolate certain records and fields in a table and save the information in a new table.

When Used

When the auditor wants a new table with only specified tables and fields included, usually when the auditor intends to do additional testing of the new table. The new table contains only the records the auditor isolated and is therefore easier to manipulate and analyze.

Examples

- Isolate customers with a credit balance in year-end accounts receivable.
- Isolate employees in a specific work department from a master file table.

TASK # 1 — Extract Certain Records to a Separate Table

Steps

▪▪▪ *Click Data → Extract to open the Extract command dialog.*

▪▪▪ *If the Record radio button is not already selected, click the button.*

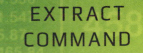

Next, you need to build a filter so that ACL knows what records you want to extract.

 Click the If button.

 Build the filter in the Expression box. See pages 6 through 9 for guidance.

 Click OK to return to the Extract command dialog.

ACL creates a new table with the extracted information. You need to provide a table name.

 Type a descriptive table name in the To box. You do not need to add the file extension: ACL automatically adds the "fil" extension. See the following illustration as an example.

 Click OK to run the command.

EXTRACT COMMAND

Command Results

The Extract command creates a new table that contains only the records that were extracted. Notice that there is a new table in the Overview window with the name of the new table you just created. In addition, the default view changes to the newly extracted table. Following is an illustration of an excerpt from an extracted table.

	Product_Number	Product_Class	Location	Product_Description	Product_Status
1	030414313	03	03	METRIC TOOL SET 3/8" DR	A
2	030414283	03	03	METRIC SOCKET SET 11 PC	A
3	030412553	03	03	6 PC OPEN END WRENCH SET	A
4	030412753	03	03	6 PC BOX END WRENCH SET	A
5	030412903	03	03	8 PC METRIC HEX KEYS	A
6	034255003	03	03	PARKER PROPANE KIT (7PC)	U
7	030364163	03	03	TAP & DIE SET 41 PIECES	A
8	030321663	03	03	SCREW DRIVER 1/8 X 4 SL	A
9	030321683	03	03	SCREW DRIVER 1/4 X 6 SL	A
10	030322303	03	03	SCREW DRIVER NO.3 PHILL	A
11	030324803	03	03	ARC JOINT PLIERS 6"	A
12	030324883	03	03	ARC JOINT PLIERS 16"	A

Locations_3_and_4

TASK # 2 — Extract Certain Fields to a Separate Table

Steps

- *Click Data → Extract to open the Extract command dialog.*
- *Click the Fields radio button if it not already selected.* All fields in the table are listed in the Extract Fields portion of the command dialog.

Extract dialog — **Main** / **More** tabs

Extract Fields...   ○ Record   ○ View   ● Fields

Name	Title	Start	Category	Length	Decimals	Type
Product_Number	Product_Num...	1	C	9	0	ASCII
Product_Description	Product_Descr...	14	C	47	0	ASCII
Product_Class	Product_Class	10	C	2	0	ASCII
Price_Date	Price_Date	90	D	10	0	DATETI
Market_Value	Market_Value	152	N	11	2	NUMER
Location	Location	12	C	2	0	ASCII
Inventory_Value_At_Cost	Inventory_Valu...	132	N	20	2	NUMER
Cost_Date	Cost_Date	71	D	10	0	DATETI

If...
To...

☑ Local   ☑ Use Output Table

OK   Cancel   Help

- *In the Extract Fields portion of the command dialog, click on the name of the field(s) on which you want to extract to a separate table. Use the Shift or Control key to select multiple fields.*
- *Click the If button. (See the top of the following page.)*

- Build the filter in the Expression box. See pages 6 through 9 for guidance.

- Click OK to return to the Extract dialog box.

- Type a descriptive table name in the To box. You do not need to add the file extension: ACL automatically adds the "fil" extension. See the illustration below as an example.

- Click OK to run the command.

Command Results

The Extract command creates a new table that includes only the fields that were extracted. Notice that there is a new table in the Overview window with the name of the new table you just created. In addition, the default view changes to the newly extracted table. Following is an illustration of a table of extracted fields for records meeting a certain condition.

	Location	Market_Value	Price_Date	Product_Class	Product_Description
1	06	8691.30	10/18/2018	07	LATEX SEMI-GLOSS ORANG
2	06	4595.40	10/18/2018	07	LATEX SEMI-GLOSS CARAMI
3	06	14785.20	10/18/2018	07	LATEX SEMI-GLOSS LILAC
4	06	12887.10	10/18/2018	07	LATEX SEMI-GLOSS APRICO
5	06	14985.00	10/18/2018	07	LATEX SEMI-GLOSS PINK
6	06	24175.80	10/18/2018	07	LATEX SEMI-GLOSS YELLOW
7	06	18681.30	10/18/2018	07	LATEX SEMI-GLOSS GREEN
8	03	7797.40	12/31/2018	03	METRIC TOOL SET 3/8" DR
9	03	15899.76	12/31/2018	03	METRIC SOCKET SET 11 PC
10	03	11186.00	12/31/2018	03	6 PC OPEN END WRENCH S

Market_Value_Report

Gaps Command
(Numeric, Character, and Date Fields)

Used For

To detect gaps in the sequence of key fields in a table.

When Used

Whenever the auditor is concerned that there are missing numbers in a sequence, usually document numbers.

Examples

- Detect missing check numbers in a check register table.
- Detect a gap in invoice number sequence in a sales transaction table.

TASK #1 — Report a List of Missing Ranges of Records

Steps

▪▪▪ *Click Analyze → Gaps to open the Gaps command dialog.* Each field in the table is listed in the Gaps command dialog.

▪▪▪ *In the Gaps On portion of the command dialog, click on the name of the field on which you want to run the Gaps command.*

▪▪▪ *Click OK to run the command.*

Command Results

The command results show all of the gap ranges detected in the field you chose. An example of Gaps command results follows.

As of:	02/16/2017 11:48:37
Command:	GAPS ON Invoice_Number PRESORT TO SCREEN
Table:	Trans

12 gap ranges detected
32 missing items

Gaps Found Between:

Gap Start (Exclusive)	Gap End (Exclusive)	Number of Missing Items
12,867	12,869	1
12,877	12,889	11
12,891	12,893	1
12,919	12,930	10
12,952	12,954	1
12,991	12,993	1
13,003	13,005	1
13,006	13,008	1
13,029	13,032	2
13,091	13,093	1
13,135	13,137	1
13,191	13,193	1

TASK #2 — Report a Listing of Individual Missing Records

Steps

▪▪▪ *Click Analyze → Gaps to open the Gaps command dialog. Each field in the table is listed in the Gaps command dialog.*

▪▪▪ *In the Gaps On portion of the command dialog, click on the name of the field on which you want to run the Gaps command.*

▪▪▪ *Click the List Missing Items radio button on the right side of the command dialog.*

The default in the Maximum Missing Items box is five. If there are more than five consecutive items missing, a range is reported rather than listing each individual item. This setting has no effect on how many missing items are reported in total; it only affects how the missing items are presented.

▪▪▪ *If you want each missing item listed separately, change this number to a high number. Otherwise, leave the default at five.*

▪▪▪ *Click OK to run the command.*

Command Results

The command results show all missing items in the field(s) you chose. An example of Gaps command results is illustrated at the top of the following page.

As of: 02/16/2017 11:51:52

Command: GAPS ON Invoice_Number PRESORT MISSING 5 TO SCREEN

Table: Trans

32 missing items

Gaps Found:

Invoice_Number	Gap Start (Inclusive)	Gap End (Inclusive)	Number of Missing Items
12,868			1
	12,878	12,888	11
12,892			1
	12,920	12,929	10
12,953			1
12,992			1
13,004			1
13,007			1
13,030			1
13,031			1
13,092			1
13,136			1
13,192			1

 Join Command

Used For

To combine information from two tables, where each table has at least one matching field, into a third table. The new table consists of matched or unmatched records from the original tables. The new table is then used like any other ACL table.

When Used

When the auditor needs information from two related tables to permit additional audit testing.

Examples

- Join a table of outstanding accounts receivable balances with a customer master file table that includes credit limits to identify customers with account balances exceeding their credit limits.
- Join a payroll transaction table with an employee master file table that includes approved gross pay per period to identify instances where employees' gross pay differs from approved amounts.

Five Requirements Before Running the Join Command

The Join command combines fields from two different tables to create a new table consisting of matched or unmatched records from the two original tables. Records are matched or unmatched based on a field that is present in both tables.

Before running the Join Command you **must complete each of the following five requirements:**

1. **Decide which two tables you want to join.** This requires audit planning to decide the information you want for the audit and the tables that include the information. **Note:** A table will not show up as available for joining as a secondary table if the primary table has already been related to that table.
2. **Decide which fields you will use to join the two tables.** The field must be the same for both tables. The fields can be character, date, or numeric, but the character field is the one most commonly used. Examples of common character fields are employee number, inventory item number, customer number, or vendor number.
3. **Decide which table will be the primary table and which the secondary.** Normally a transaction table is defined as the primary table and the related master file table becomes the secondary table.

4. **Satisfy the six primary and secondary table rules.** See pages 56 and 57 of this book for the six rules.

5. **Decide which of five join options to select for the join.** Each option accomplishes something different. Deciding the appropriate option requires careful planning. Selecting the wrong option can result in reaching wrong audit conclusions. See pages 57 through 60 in this book for guidance in selecting an option.

Join Steps

After the initial five steps are completed, you are ready to start the Join command.

> ⊞ *Open the primary table.*

> *Click Data → Join to open the Join command dialog.*

> *Use the Secondary Table drop-down list arrow to select the secondary table.*

> *In the Primary Keys section of the command dialog, click on the name of the primary key field.*

> *In the Secondary Keys section of the command dialog, click on the name of the secondary key field.*

Next, ACL needs to know which fields to include in the joined table. The fields you select depend on the objective of your testing. Include all fields that you are interested in testing in the join.

■■■ *Click the Primary Fields button to open the Selected Fields window. Either double-click on each field to include it in the joined table or use the Add All button to select all fields.*

■■■ *Click OK to return to the Main tab.*

■■■ *Click the Secondary Field button to open the Selected Fields window. Either double-click on each field to include it in the joined table or use the Add All button to select all fields.*

■■■ *Click OK to return to the Main tab.*

■■■ *Click the Presort Secondary Table box.*

■■■ *Click the More tab.*

The next step is to select the appropriate Join option from the five options described on pages 57 through 60. Refer to these pages when choosing among the five options.

- *Use the radio buttons and/or check boxes to select the appropriate Join option. You may select only one of two radio buttons: Matched Primary Records for options 1 through 4 or Unmatched Primary Records for option 5. (Note: You will not use Many-To-Many Matched Records in this project.) If you decide on option 2 or 3, select Matched Primary Records and check the appropriate box — Include All Primary Records or Include All Secondary Records. If you decide on option 4, select Matched Primary Records and check both boxes.*

- *Click the Main tab to return to the main portion of the Join command dialog.*

- *Type a meaningful table name in the To box. It is helpful to include at least part of each table name from the primary and secondary tables. An example of a meaningful joined table name is "SalesTrans_Join_InvMaster."*

- *Click OK to join the two tables.*

Command Results

The Join command creates a new table that contains only the records for the joined table. Notice that there is a new table in the Overview window with the name of the new table you just created. In addition, the default view changes to the new joined table. You can move the columns of the joined table to manipulate the joined data for further analysis. An excerpt from a joined table follows.

	Vendor_Number	Invoice_Number	Invoice_Date	Invoice_Amount	Vendor_Name	Vendor_Number	Vendor_Name
1	10025	234056	09/30/2018	486.00	Mitchell Ent.	10025	Mitchell Ent.
2	10025	230592	09/30/2018	850.58	Mitchell Ent.	10025	Mitchell Ent.
3	10025	239215	09/30/2018	278.04	Mitchell Ent.	10025	Mitchell Ent.
4	10025	237936	01/31/2018	56767.20	Mitchell Ent.	10025	Mitchell Ent.
5	10025	232195	11/14/2018	965.77	Mitchell Ent.	10025	Mitchell Ent.
6	10101	4517604	10/30/2018	154.00	Breathed & Company	10101	Breathed & Company
7	10101	4514742	10/15/2018	50.40	Breathed & Company	10101	Breathed & Company
8	10101	4516050	07/31/2018	486.64	Breathed & Company	10101	Breathed & Company
9	10134	71073	09/29/2018	883.00	Stars Trading	10134	Stars Trading
10	10134	74841	11/12/2018	18883.34	Stars Trading	10134	Stars Trading
11	10134	70075	04/09/2018	467.40	Stars Trading	10134	Stars Trading
12	10134	78025	09/30/2018	1823.68	Stars Trading	10134	Stars Trading
13	10134	70936	02/14/2018	561.20	Stars Trading	10134	Stars Trading

AP_Trans_Join_Vendor

Note: After the Join is completed the new table can be joined with another table if they both meet the six rules for a Join shown below.

Six Primary and Secondary Table Rules (Requirement 4 on page 54)

Each of the following rules must be satisfied before running a Join command. When you are running Join more than once on the same two tables, it is not necessary to satisfy the rules after the first join. The way to satisfy each rule, except the first two, is shown in italics.

1. The two input tables must be in the same ACL project.
2. Only two tables can be joined at one time.

3. Both tables must contain a common field to be used to join the tables. *Use Table Layout in both tables.*

4. The key field must be the same length in both tables. *Use Table Layout in both tables.*

5. ⓕ The key field in both tables should be tested for blanks. *Use a filter on the key field in both tables.*

6. The key field in both tables should be tested for duplicates. *Use the Duplicate command on both tables. If there are extensive duplicates use the Summarize command and save the summarized data into a new table.*

Five Join Options (Requirement 5 on page 54)

The auditor must select one of the five join options each time the Join command is used. The following provides guidance in selecting the option. For each option, a figure is used to depict the records selected in the option. Understanding each of the five figures is critical to selecting the best option.

To illustrate each option the following example is used:

Primary Table – Monthly sales
　　Fields–Inventory item sold and unit selling price

Secondary Table – Inventory master file
　　Fields–Inventory item number and unit selling price

The common field used to join the two tables is the inventory item number field. In all cases the auditor selects the item number and the unit selling price from each table for the joined table.

Option 1, Matched Primary Records Join: Creates one output record for every primary table record that has a match in the secondary table.

Matched Primary Records

As can be seen from the diagram, the joined table includes inventory items included in both tables. The joined table also includes the selling price from both the primary and secondary tables for those items where there is a match. The auditor can create a filter on the new table comparing the selling prices to identify those with differences.

Also, as can be seen in the diagram, the matched primary records join will not include either of the following:

- An inventory item sold that was not in the master file.
- A master file inventory item that was not sold during the sales month.

For most audits, the absence of the first exclusion would be a serious audit deficiency.

Option 2, Matched Records, Includes All Primary Records Join: Creates one output record for every primary table record that has a match in the secondary table and an additional record for every unmatched primary table record.

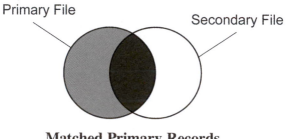

Primary File   Secondary File

Matched Primary Records
Includes All Primary Records

For this example, as can be seen from the diagram, the joined table includes inventory items included in both tables (dark shading) plus the unmatched record from the primary table (light shading). The unmatched records are inventory items in the primary table that are not in the secondary table. These are of great interest to the auditor in this case because they represent items included as being sold for which there is no record in the master file table.

A filter on the new table comparing the selling prices will identify those with differences. Inventory items in the primary table that are not in the secondary table will show up as zeros in the joined table.

As can be seen in the diagram, this join would not include a master file inventory item that was not sold in the sales month. In many audits, this is the ideal type of join.

Option 3, Matched Primary Records, Includes All Secondary Records Join: Creates an output record for every primary table record that has a match in the secondary table, plus one record for every unmatched secondary table record.

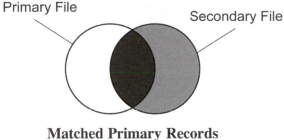

Matched Primary Records
Includes All Secondary Records

For this example, as can be seen from the diagram, the joined table includes inventory items included in both tables (dark shading) plus the unmatched records from the secondary table (light shading). In most audits the auditor would not be interested in the inventory items in the master file not sold in a certain month.

A filter on the joined table comparing the selling prices will identify those with differences. Inventory items in the secondary table that are not in the primary table will show up as blanks or zeros, depending on the field type in the output table.

As can be seen in the diagram, this join will not include an inventory item sold that was not in the master file. For most audits, the absence of this exclusion would be a serious audit deficiency.

Option 4, Matched Primary; Includes all Primary; Includes all Secondary Join: Creates an output record for every primary table record that has a match in the secondary table, plus one record for every unmatched primary table record and one record for every unmatched secondary table record.

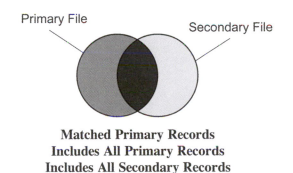

Matched Primary Records
Includes All Primary Records
Includes All Secondary Records

For this example, as can be seen from the diagram above, the joined table includes inventory items and selling prices included in both tables (dark shading), the unmatched records from the primary table (medium shading), plus the unmatched records from the secondary table (light shading).

A filter on the new table comparing the selling prices will identify those with differences.

As can be seen in the diagram on the previous page, this join accounts for all inventory items sold and all inventory items included in the master file table. This is the safest type of join because it includes all matched and unmatched records from both tables. But, there may be a large number of records in which the auditor has no interest. Typically, for that reason, the auditor does not choose this option often.

Option 5, Unmatched Primary Records Join: Creates one output record for every primary table record that does not have a match in the secondary table.

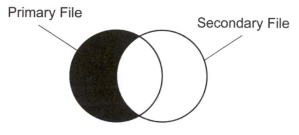

Unmatched Primary Records

For this example, as can be seen from the diagram, the joined table includes inventory records in the primary table that are not in the secondary. This join is useful if the only objective is to test for items sold that are not included in the master file. If the auditor also wants to compare unit costs on both tables, this join would not be sufficient.

Relations Command

Used For

To establish a relationship between two or more tables. The relationship is maintained through a common field. Unlike the Join command, the Relations command links the tables together without combining them into a new physical table. The Relations command permits the access of data spanning multiple tables.

When Used

The auditor needs information from two or more related tables to permit additional audit testing. The Relations command permits the auditor to access multiple related tables.

Examples

- Recalculate commission expenses for the year by relating a commission expense table to a table containing commission rates by product number.
- Relate a sales transaction table to an inventory master file table, using product number as the key field. Recalculate sales amount for each inventory item sold by accessing the master file table sales price and multiplying it by the quantity sold from the sales transaction file table.

Requirements Before Running the Relations Command

1. **Decide which tables you want to relate.**
2. **Decide which table will be the parent table and which one or ones will be the child.** Normally the parent table is a transaction table and the child table is one that is related to the transaction file, such as a master file table. Note: The parent table is equivalent to the primary table in the Join command and the child table is equivalent to the secondary table. Each parent table can be related to up to seventeen child tables.
3. **Decide which field or fields you will use to relate the table or tables.** Any given field must be the same for the parent table and at least one child table. A second or third parent table field can be matched to a child table if there is a child table with the same field.
4. **Satisfy the five Relations command rules.** See page 65 of this book for the five rules.

Steps

After the four requirements are satisfied, you are ready to start the Relations command.

              Open the parent table.

              Click Data → Relate to open the Relations command dialog.

A box appears in the top left corner of the Relations command dialog. This box represents the parent table and each field in the parent table is listed in the box.

              Click the Add Table button. The Add Table window opens with a list of all tables in the current ACL project.

              Double-click on the table you want to select as the child table.

              Click the key field from the parent table and drag it to the key field of the child table.

As shown below, a line appears that connects the two tables using the common key field. The common key field does not have to have the same name in each table, but each must contain the same information and be the same field type and size.

▪▮▮ *Carefully review the relationship established in the previous step. To delete a key field relation, right-click on the line that connects the two tables and select the Delete option. To delete a child table box from the Relations command dialog entirely, right-click on the child table box, and then click Remove Table.*

▪▮▮ *Repeat the previous four steps for each child table you want to relate to the parent table.*

▪▮▮ *Click Finish to create the relationship(s) between the parent table and the child table(s).*

After a relationship has been established between the parent table and a child table, the following tasks are now possible:

- Select fields from the child table for inclusion in the view of the parent table.
- Create a filter in the parent table using fields from the child table. You can use filters after relating the tables to create results equivalent to Matched Primary, Matched Primary; Includes All Primary, and Unmatched Primary.
- Issue commands in the parent table using fields from the child table.

An example of the use of the related tables is illustrated below:

▪▮▮ *Follow the preceding steps to relate the Payroll table (parent) and the Empmast table (child). The common field is Employee_Number. Assume all five requirements are satisfied.*

▪▮▮ *After the relations command is completed, open the Payroll table and create a filter to determine if there are employee numbers on the Payroll table that are not included on the Empmast table. Do the following:*

1. *Open the Edit view filter window by clicking on the Edit View Filter button* (fx).

2. *Click on the drop-down box under "From Table" on the bottom left of the screen.* Observe that the two items in the table window are Payroll and Empmast.

3. *Alternately click on each table name in the From Table box and observe the change in the Table layout.* When the Payroll table is in the From Table drop-down box, the fields in the Payroll table are in the Table Layout. The Table Layout changes when the Empmast table is in the From Table drop-down box. This is the way ACL relates tables using the Relations command.

4. *Make sure the Payroll table is in the From Table drop-down box. Then create the first part of the expression in the filter window by double-clicking Employee_Number, then the operator <>. Now click on Empmast in the From Table drop-down box. Complete the expression by double-clicking on the employee number. The expression should look as follows: Employee_Number <> Empmast.Employee_Number. Then click OK.* Your results should look like the illustration that follows.

Payroll

EMPLOYEE_NUMBER <> Empmast.Employer_Number

	EMPLOYEE_NUMBER	WORK_DEPT_	GROSS_PAY	TAXABLE_AMOUNT	NET_PAY	PAY_DATE	CHECK_NUMBER
8	000108	E21	2179.17	435.83	1743.34	09/15/2018	12353
9	000109	E21	2179.17	435.83	1743.34	09/15/2018	12354
	<< End of File >>						

Five Relations Command Rules (Requirement 4 on page 61)

Each of the following must be satisfied before running the Relations command. The way to satisfy each rule, except the first two, is shown in italics.

1. All tables being related must be in the same ACL project.

2. The parent table must have a key field in common with each child table. The link does not need to be the same for each child.

3. The key field in the parent table must have the same length, justification, and case (upper, lower, or proper) as the common field in a child table. *Use Table Layout in both tables.*

4. ⓕ Key fields in all tables should be tested for blanks. If blanks exist in both the parent table and a child table, they will be linked together, but might not actually represent comparable data. *Use a filter on the key field in both tables.*

5. Key field in all tables should be tested for duplicates. If duplicate records are found in a child table, only the first record will be selected. Duplicates in the parent table are acceptable, but still need to be noted for analysis. *Use the Duplicate Command on both tables. If there are extensive duplicates use the Summarize command and save the summarized data into a new table.*

Sample Command – MUS Sampling

Used For

To select a random sample of monetary units, usually dollars, from a population or subpopulation. ACL selects random monetary units, but the output is a record that includes the random monetary unit.

When Used

Whenever the auditor wants to select an MUS sample using ACL. Note: If you want to select a random sample of records instead of monetary units, see Sampling Command – Records Sampling.

Examples

- Select a random sample of accounts receivable for confirmation.
- Select a random sample of inventory items to perform price testing.

Calculating the Sample Size and MUS Sampling Interval

To calculate a monetary unit sample, the auditor enters four items:

1. The desired confidence level for the test. Typical confidence levels are 90% or 95%, but can be lower depending on the required degree of assurance from the test.
2. The dollar amount of the population, which can be determined using the Total command.
3. Materiality, which is usually tolerable misstatement for the sampling application.
4. The dollar amount of errors expected in the testing. Auditors generally expect little or no error when using MUS. However, the auditor may allow for a small amount of expected error so that the detection of one or a few small misstatements does not garner unacceptable test results.

When using the MUS Sampling command, the table must be organized consistently with your sampling needs. For example, if you wish to sample accounts receivable balances rather than invoices, a file of sales invoices may need to be summarized into a table of total accounts receivable by customer before selecting a sample for confirmation. *Do not skip this step if the instructions indicate you are to sample individual customer balances rather than individual outstanding invoices.* However, because the sampling unit in MUS is individual monetary units (dollars), a sample can be drawn from balances or invoices.

When using MUS Sampling, adjustments are often made to the population to determine samples size.

- The $ value of key items (records) are often excluded. Key items are amounts exceeding a dollar limit that the auditor decides must be audited. An example is inventory items exceeding $10,000.
- The $ value of items the auditor decides not to include in the sample. An example is negative values in accounts receivable.

The auditor can include the key items in the sample size determination, but this will usually result in a larger sample size. Further, auditing standards require that these key items be tested. For this reason, auditors find it more convenient to exclude them from the population to be sampled and test the key items separately.

Illustration of Calculating the Sample Size and MUS Sampling Interval

Following is an example from an audit program: Select a sample of inventory items from the Inventory table in the Sample_Project for physical examination. The auditor's desired confidence level is 90%, and tolerable misstatement (materiality) is $50,000. Therefore, key items are any inventory items with a total cost value more than or equal to $50,000. Do not include negative balances in the sample. The auditor expects total errors in the population of $1,500.

Before using the Sampling command to determine sample size, the auditor does the following:

1. Determine the total inventory value at cost in the Inventory table using ACL ($680,479.94).
2. Filter out the key items. (One item totaling $100,800 has a balance exceeding $50,000.)
3. Determine the total amount of negative balances using a filter. (The total is $–13,882.)

Note that the two filters can be combined. After applying these two filters, the remaining inventory value at cost is $593,561.94. Although not required, it is recommended that the filtered table be saved as a separate table since it represents the population to be sampled.

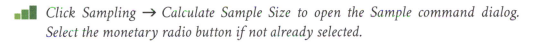 *Click Sampling → Calculate Sample Size to open the Sample command dialog. Select the monetary radio button if not already selected.*

4. Calculate the required sample size on the adjusted population using the indicated parameters.

If you completed the steps as indicated, you should calculate a sample size of 28 and a sampling interval of $20,619.04. Note that the maximum tainting is 7.27%, which is the expected number of errors divided by the sampling interval ($1,500/$20,619.04). If the auditor finds an error that is greater than 7.27% of the account balance, the results of the sample will be considered unacceptable.

Size					X
Main	**Output**				
● Monetary		○ Record			
Confidence			90		
Population			593561.94		
Materiality			50000		
Expected Total Errors			1500		
Results					
				Calculate	
Sample Size				28	
Interval				20,619.04	
Maximum Tolerable Taintings (%)				7.27	
		OK	Cancel	Help	

 Click OK to close the Size window.

Sample Records

To select the sample items, use the following steps.

 Click Sampling → Sample.

Sample				X
Main	**More**			
		Sample Type		
Sample On...		● MUS	○ Record	
Inventory_Value_At_Cost				▾
Sample Parameters				
● Fixed Interval	Interval			
○ Cell	Start			
○ Random	Cutoff			
Algorithm	Mersenne Twister	▾	Size...	
If...				
To...				
☑ Local	☑ Use Output Table			
		OK	Cancel	Help

▪▪▪ *Click the MUS radio button for Sample Type and the Fixed Interval radio button for Sample Parameter unless they are already selected as defaults.*

▪▪▪ *Click the Sample On box and select the field on which you want to select the sample.*

▪▪▪ *Click OK to return to the main command dialog.*

▪▪▪ *Enter the interval for the population in the Interval box as determined when the sample size was determined.*

▪▪▪ *Enter any number between 1 and the length of the interval in the Start box to assure a random start. (Use 4371 for the example.)*

▪▪▪ *Enter an output table name in the To box to save the random selection.*

Use the Cutoff box for key items that will be automatically included in the sample if you have not already filtered them from the population. Similarly, use the If button if you plan to restrict the random selection to certain population items, such as positive account balances, if you have not already applied a filter to exclude them from the population to be sampled. The illustration below assumes that the key items and excluded items have already been filtered.

Click the More tab, check the No Repeats box.

 Click OK to run the Sample MUS command.

Command Results

The output table includes the sample selected in records, not monetary units. An example of an MUS sampling table created with the Sampling command for the example follows:

	Product_Number	Product_Class	Location	Product_Description	Product_Status	Unit_Cost	Cost_Date
1	070104347	07	06	LATEX SEMI-GLOSS ORANGE	A	6.87	10/10/2018
2	070104677	07	06	LATEX SEMI-GLOSS APRICOT	A	6.87	10/10/2018
3	070104327	07	06	LATEX SEMI-GLOSS YELLOW	A	6.87	10/10/2018
4	070104377	07	06	LATEX SEMI-GLOSS GREEN	A	6.87	10/10/2018
5	030412553	03	03	6 PC OPEN END WRENCH SET	A	11.53	09/30/2018
6	030324883	03	03	ARC JOINT PLIERS 16"	A	9.40	03/30/2018
7	030303343	03	03	STRAIGHT CLAW HAMMER	A	8.83	08/10/2018
8	030309373	03	03	HEAVY DUTY BRACE	A	10.12	10/12/2018
9	030302303	03	03	MITRE BOX 21"	A	41.23	10/12/2018
10	090507811	09	04	50' RUBBER HOSE	A	8.08	10/03/2018
11	090509931	09	04	OSCILLATING SPRINKLER	A	5.84	08/10/2018
12	090584072	09	04	22" SELF-PROPELLED MOW	A	173.80	08/10/2018
13	090585322	09	04	18" REEL MOWER	A	137.80	08/10/2018
14	010102840	01	01	PRESSURE COOKER 8QT	A	39.40	11/19/2018
15	010135060	01	01	192 OZ DUTCH OVEN	A	27.60	11/19/2018
16	052484415	05	05	PLYWOOD 4X8X 1/2 GIS	A	5.20	01/10/2018
17	052504005	05	05	5/16 SHEATHING	A	3.94	09/10/2018
18	080102618	08	02	1/2" SOFT TUBING 30'COIL	A	16.80	10/20/2018
19	080102628	08	02	R161D TUBING 1/2" -12'	A	7.00	10/20/2018
20	080126008	08	02	1/2" CPVC PLASTIC PIPE	A	2.41	06/30/2018
21	080935298	08	02	HYDROMOULD SWING-SPOUT	A	21.12	06/15/2018
22	024106512	02	02	HOCKEY PANTS	A	14.80	02/05/2018
23	060102096	06	02	SEVILLE ENTRANCE SET BR	A	38.70	09/11/2018
24	060102086	06	02	COLONIAL ENTRANCE SET BR	A	32.08	10/20/2018
25	060217066	06	02	ALUMINUM DOOR	A	87.40	09/09/2018
26	040225934	04	03	MASONRY DRILL SET	A	5.10	09/14/2018
27	040232194	04	03	12 SP AUTO SCROLLER SAW	A	59.60	12/01/2018
28	040241314	04	03	ROUT-A-FORM PANTOGRAPH	A	18.70	01/01/2018
29	040277154	04	03	ADJUSTABLE DADO	A	36.57	08/09/2018

Inventory_MUS_Sample

<< End of File >>

The auditor would then perform applicable tests on the resulting sample. For example, the auditor might perform pricing tests by relating the prices used in valuing inventory with a master file of inventory prices. If the MUS sample is for accounts receivable, the resulting output table can be used to prepare confirmations by relating the sample output table to the customer master file table and pulling the name, address, city, state, and zip code information into the sample table. The information can then be used for preparation of confirmations for mailing.

The interval approach illustrated is only one approach to selecting an MUS sample. The auditor can also choose to select random dollars or random dollars in an interval (cell method). Because these methods are less common in practice, they are not illustrated here.

Evaluate Error in an MUS Sample

To evaluate the errors in MUS, use the following steps.

 Click Sampling → Evaluate Error. (See the illustration at the top of the following page.)

Evaluate

Main | Output

- (•) Monetary   Confidence
- ( ) Record   Interval

Item amount, Error

Errors

OK   Cancel   Help

▪▪▪ *Click the Monetary radio button if it has not already been selected.*

▪▪▪ *Enter the confidence level for the test.* (90 in this example.)

▪▪▪ *Enter the length of the sampling interval.* (Use 20,619.04 for the example.)

▪▪▪ *Enter each error in the format Item Amount, Error.* For example, assume that a sampled inventory item with a total cost of $5,000 had an overstatement error of $300, and another inventory item with a total cost of $7,500 had an overstatement error of $1,640. These would be entered as follows:

> 5000, 300
> 7500, 1640

Evaluate

Main | Output

- (•) Monetary   Confidence   90
- ( ) Record   Interval   20619.04

Item amount, Error

Errors   5000, 300
         7500, 1640|

OK   Cancel   Help

▪▪▪ *Click OK to complete run the command.*

Command Results

The output table for the evaluation of sample results is included below.

As of: 02/16/2017 15:18:14

Command: EVALUATE MONETARY CONFIDENCE 90 ERRORLIMIT 5000, 300,7500, 1640 INTERVAL 20619.04 TO SCREEN

Confidence: 90, **Interval:** 20619

	Item	Error	Most Likely Error	Upper Error Limit
Basic Precision				47,630.00
	7,500.00	1,640.00	4,508.70	7,123.75
	5,000.00	300.00	1,237.14	1,781.48
Totals			5,745.84	56,535.23

The first line labeled Basic Precision is the allowance for sampling risk assuming no misstatements are found in the sample. The following two lines in the table present the two sample misstatements in order of percentage misstatement. The most likely error is the projected misstatement, calculated as the percentage misstatement times the length of the sampling interval ($1,640/$7,500 x $20,619.04 = $4,508.70). The last column is the projected error plus the incremental allowance for sampling risk. The auditor compares the upper error limit to the tolerable misstatement for the sampling application to conclude on the acceptability of the population.

Sample Command – Record Sampling

Used For

To select a random sample of records of a specified size from a population or subpopulation.

When Used

Whenever the auditor wants to select a random sample of records using ACL. If you want a random sample of dollars instead of records, see Sample Command – MUS Sampling on pages 66 through 72.

Examples

- Select a random sample of purchase transactions to perform a test of control for proper authorization.
- Select a random sample of inventory items to perform price testing.

When using the Record Sampling command, the table must be organized consistently with your sampling needs. For example, when sampling sales transactions the auditor may want to exclude sales returns. Use a filter before running the Sampling command and extract the filtered data to a new table from which you wish to sample.

Illustration of Calculating the Sample Size for Record Sampling

Following is an example from an audit program: Select a sample of accounts receivable transactions from the Trans table in the AR_Test_Scripts subfolder in the Accounts_Receivable_Audit folder in the Sample_Project for control testing. The auditor's desired confidence level is 90%, the tolerable exception rate is 8%, and the excepted exception rate is zero. The following information is needed to determine sample size using record sampling:

1. Specify the desired confidence level for the test.
2. Enter the number of records in the population. (Identified from record count at the bottom of the screen.)
3. Enter the upper error limit (tolerable exception rate).
4. Enter the expected error rate.

   Click Sampling → Calculate Sample Size to open the Sample command dialog. Select the record radio button if not already selected.

5. Calculate the required sample size on the adjusted population using the indicated parameters.

Based on the sample parameters, you should calculate a sample size of 29.

 Click OK to close the Size window.

Select Sample

For record sampling, the auditor normally desires a random sample of the population items.

 Click Sampling → Sample to open the Sample command dialog.

Click the Record radio button for Sample Type and the Random radio button for Sample Parameters unless they are already selected as defaults.

 Type the desired sample size for the population stratum in the Size box and any seed number between 1 and 9,999 in the Seed box to assure a random start. Use 2550 for the example.

 Enter an output table name in the To box to save the random selection.

Click OK to run the Sample Records Command.

Command Results

The output table includes the sample selected in records. An example of a typical record sampling table created with the Sampling command is illustrated at the top of the following page.

Trans_Random_Sample

	Cust_Number	Invoice_Date	Due_Date	Ref_No	Trans_Type	Trans_Amount
1	065003	08/31/2018	11/29/2018	213248	IN	874.97
2	516372	08/31/2018	09/30/2018	213285	CN	-80.74
3	262001	09/15/2018	03/14/2018	213436	IN	1189.11
4	925007	09/28/2018	03/27/2018	213644	IN	1189.11
5	501657	10/06/2018	11/05/2018	213755	CN	-18.58
6	778088	10/14/2018	01/12/2018	213823	IN	580.87
7	262001	10/16/2018	11/15/2018	213837	IN	590.96
8	811002	10/22/2018	11/21/2018	213910	CN	-10.90
9	230575	10/22/2018	11/21/2018	213920	IN	24.86
10	065003	10/23/2018	11/22/2018	213925	IN	1108.74
11	516372	11/02/2018	12/02/2018	214003	IN	520.87
12	262001	11/04/2018	12/04/2018	214020	IN	377.37
13	207275	11/04/2018	12/04/2018	214040	IN	1546.15
14	262001	11/05/2018	05/04/2018	214036	IN	1717.61
15	065003	11/09/2018	02/07/2018	214067	IN	810.37
16	264629	11/09/2018	12/09/2018	214068	IN	146.76
17	297397	11/18/2018	12/18/2018	214139	IN	48.92
18	262001	11/19/2018	12/19/2018	214149	IN	903.51
19	925007	11/19/2018	12/19/2018	214152	IN	1723.45
20	176437	11/23/2018	12/23/2018	214184	CN	-182.08
21	376005	11/26/2018	12/26/2018	214193	IN	526.05
22	925007	11/30/2018	12/30/2018	214219	IN	1495.75
23	516372	12/01/2018	12/31/2018	214236	IN	1379.43
24	516372	12/03/2018	01/02/2018	214270	CN	-33.81
25	176437	12/02/2018	11/19/2018	213872	PM	-1203.07
26	836004	12/08/2018	01/07/2018	214307	IN	871.55
27	501657	12/04/2018	10/21/2018	213572	PM	54.66
28	376005	12/09/2018	01/08/2018	214359	IN	514.62
29	297397	12/09/2018	01/08/2018	214367	IN	539.96

Evaluate Errors in Record Sampling

To evaluate the errors in record sampling, use the following steps.

Click Sampling → Evaluate Error.

■■■ *Click the Record radio button if it has not already been selected.*

■■■ *Enter the confidence level for the test.* (90 in this example.)

■■■ *Enter the sample size.* (Use 29 for the example.)

■■■ *Enter the number of errors.* (Use 0 for the example.)

■■■ *Click OK to run the command.*

ACL calculates the upper error limit. Note that the limit will be less than the tolerable rate if the error rate in the sample is equal to or less than the error rate used to plan the sample if the auditor selects a sample size equal to or larger than the sample size determined in the planning the sample.

As of: 02/16/2017 14:55:19

Command: EVALUATE RECORD CONFIDENCE 90 SIZE 29 ERRORLIMIT 0 TO SCREEN

Confidence: 90, Sample Size: 29, Number of Errors: 0

The upper error limit frequency is: 7.97%

Sequence Command
(Numeric, Character, and Date Fields)

Used For

- To determine if key fields in a table are in sequential order. Note: ACL does not consider gaps or duplicates to be sequence errors. See pages 37 and 49, respectively, for the Duplicates and Gaps commands.
- To determine sequential order for tables that will be joined with other tables. (See the Join Command section on page 53).

When Used

Whenever the auditor is concerned that there are gaps in a sequence of numbers, usually document numbers.

Examples

- Identify exceptions to the sequence of invoice numbers in a sales file.
- Identify exceptions to the sequence of check numbers in a payroll transactions file.

Steps

Click Analyze → Sequence to open the Sequence command dialog. Each field in the current table is listed in the Sequence command dialog.

▪▪▪ *Click the Sequence On button.* The Selected Fields window opens and a list of fields appears in the Available Fields portion of the window.

▪▪▪ *Double-click on the name of the field(s) on which you want to run the Sequence command. Make sure they are in the Selected Fields box. To select all fields, click the Add All button.*

After a field is selected, the name of the field is inserted into the Selected Fields portion of the window, along with an upward pointing arrow. The default for the Sequence command is to test the sequence in ascending order. To change to descending order, click the upward arrow and it changes to a downward arrow. The sequence is then checked in descending order.

▪▪▪ *If necessary, change the sequence order to descending.*

▪▪▪ *Click OK to return to the Main tab of the Sequence command dialog.*

The default number of sequence errors reported by ACL is ten. To change the number, complete the following steps:

▪▪▪ *Click the More tab and change the number in the error limit box to the number of sequence errors you want reported.* If you want to know all sequence errors in the entire table, use the total number of records in the table.

▪▪▪ *Click OK to run the command.*

Command Results

The command results show the number of sequence errors found, up to the error limit chosen (default is ten). ACL lists the record number and key field for each sequence error reported. Following is an illustration of Sequence command results.

As of: 02/16/2017 12:26:55
Command: SEQUENCE ON Invoice_Number ERRORLIMIT 10 TO SCREEN
Table: Trans

5 sequence errors detected

Sequence:

Record Number	Invoice_Number
32	12893
69	12930
132	12993
229	13093
330	13193

Sort Command
(Numeric, Character, and Date Fields)

Used For

To change the sequence of a table in ascending or descending order based on specified key fields and save the information into a new table.

When Used

When the auditor wants a new table sorted differently from the original table. Typically the auditor intends to do additional ACL testing on the new table.

Examples

- Sort a year-end accounts receivable table by date of outstanding invoices.
- Sort a payroll transaction file by work department.

Steps

Click Data → Sort to open the Sort command dialog. All fields in the table are listed in the Sort command dialog.

Click the Sort On box to open the Selected Fields window.

Double-click on the name of the field on which you want to sort the table.

To change the sorting order from ascending (default) to descending, click on the arrow next to the field name in the Selected Fields portion of the window. If ascending order is fine, skip this step. An example of a completed window is illustrated at the top of the following page.

Click OK to return to the Sort command dialog.

The Sort command produces an output table that has been physically reordered based on the specified key fields. Provide a meaningful name for the new table. For example, the following name could be used for an inventory table sorted by product number: Inventory_Sort_By_ProdNum.

Type a descriptive table name in the To box. Do not add the file extension: ACL automatically adds the "fil" extension. An example of a completed window follows. Observe that it is also possible to do a conditional sort by use of the If button.

Click OK to run the command.

Command Results

The Sort command creates a new sorted data table. Notice that there is a new table in the Overview window with the name of the new table you just created. In addition, the default view changes to the new sorted table. Following is an illustration of an excerpt from a sorted table.

⊞ Inventory_Sort_By_ProdNum

	Invoice_Number	Product_Number	Product_Class	Quantity	Invoice_Amount	Invoice_Date
1	12876	010102710	01	7	41.93	01/29/2018
2	13049	010102710	01	4	23.96	07/29/2018
3	12912	010102840	01	126	4964.40	03/01/2018
4	13013	010102840	01	135	5319.00	06/18/2018
5	13193	010102840	01	40	1576.00	12/22/2018
6	12897	010134420	01	708	2208.96	02/12/2018
7	12932	010134420	01	100	312.00	03/24/2018
8	12946	010134420	01	2	6.24	04/06/2018
9	12962	010134420	01	123	383.76	04/22/2018
10	13008	010134420	01	324	1010.88	06/12/2018
11	13025	010134420	01	617	1975.04	06/30/2018
12	13037	010134420	01	4	12.48	07/10/2018
13	13074	010134420	01	26	81.12	08/26/2018
14	13112	010134420	01	209	652.08	10/06/2018
15	13159	010134420	01	105	327.60	11/26/2018
16	13195	010134420	01	44	137.28	12/25/2018

Statistics Command

(Numeric and Date Fields)

Used For

- To identify characteristics in client data files to better understand the data being audited.
- To identify unusual characteristics in numeric and date fields for the entire table or for fields that meet certain conditions.

When Used

Typically used immediately after the Verify, Count, and Total commands to identify such things as positive and negative totals and averages in a table, a designated number of the largest and smallest values, and the date bounds in a table.

Examples

- Calculate the average number of days outstanding in an accounts receivable table.
- Calculate the average outstanding balance for customers in the 61–90 day category in an accounts receivable table.
- Identify the most and least current dates in a sales transaction table.

TASK # 1 — Generate Statistics for a Numeric or Date Field

Steps

Click *Analyze* → *Statistics to open the Statistics command dialog.* (See the illustration that follows.)

Name	Title	Start	Category	Length	Decimals	Ty
Unit_Cost	Unit_Cost	62	N	9	2	N
Sales_Price	Sales_Price	81	N	9	2	N
Reorder_Point	Reorder_Point	110	N	10	0	N
Quantity_On_Order	Quantity_On_...	120	N	12	0	N
Quantity_On_Hand	Quantity_On_...	100	N	10	0	N
Price_Date	Price_Date	90	D	10	0	D.
Market_Value	Market_Value	152	N	11	2	N
Inventory_Value_At_Cost	Inventory_Valu...	132	N	20	2	N
Cost_Date	Cost_Date	71	D	10	0	D.

▪▪▪ *Select the numeric or date field(s) you want to generate statistics on by clicking on the line(s) containing the field name(s). Use the Shift or Control key to select more than one field.*

▪▪▪ *Use the More tab to request a different number of high/low transactions than the default of five.*

Statistics

| Main | More | Output |

To
- ● Screen
- ○ Graph
- ○ Print
- ○ File

As

File Type   ASCII Text File ▼

[Name...]

☐ Local

Optional

[Header...]

[Footer...]

[OK] [Cancel] [Help]

▪▪▪ *Click OK to run the command.*

Command Results

An example of command results for a Statistics command follows.

As of:	02/16/2017 13:08:09
Command:	STATISTICS ON Unit_Cost TO SCREEN
Table:	Inventory

Unit_Cost

	Number	Total	Average
Range	-	388.07	-
Positive	149	2,642.35	17.73
Negative	3	-16.88	-5.63
Zeros	0	-	-
Totals	152	2,625.47	17.27
Abs Value	-	2,659.23	-

Highest	Lowest
381.20	-6.87
173.80	-6.80
155.80	-3.21
137.80	0.01
87.40	0.03

Notice that the command results show the following information for the numeric field(s) selected:

- Number of records with positive, negative, and zero values in the field(s) selected.
- Total unit or dollar value of records with positive, negative, and zero values in the field(s) selected.
- Average unit or dollar value of records with positive, negative, and zero values in the field(s) selected.
- The absolute value and range of the unit or dollar value in the field(s) selected.
- The five highest and five lowest values in the field(s) selected (default is five; a different high/low number can be selected).

Similar information is shown in the command results for date fields, but the only meaningful calculations are the five highest (most recent) dates, five lowest (oldest) dates, and possibly the average date.

TASK #2 — Generate Statistics for Numeric or Date Fields that Meet Certain Conditions

The Statistics command can also be used to generate statistical calculations for records that meet certain criteria.

Steps

$\frac{\Sigma}{\mu\sigma}$ *Click Analyze → Statistics to open the Statistics command dialog.*

Select the numeric or date field(s) you want to generate statistics on by clicking on the line containing the field name(s). Note: Use the Shift and/or Control key to select more than one field.

 Click the If button.

Build the filter in the Expression box. See pages 6 through 9 for guidance.

Use the More tab to request a different number of high/low transactions than the default of five.

Click OK to run the command.

Command Results

The command results show the same information for a conditional Statistics command as the results for a general Statistics command, except that the information is only for the records specified in the filter. The following is an example of command results for a conditional statistics command.

As of: 02/16/2017 13:12:52

Command: STATISTICS ON Unit_Cost IF Location="03" TO SCREEN

Table: Inventory

Condition: Location="03" (37 records matched)

Unit_Cost

	Number	Total	Average
Range	-	380.47	-
Positive	37	1,026.97	27.76
Negative	0	0.00	0.00
Zeros	0	-	-
Totals	37	1,026.97	27.76
Abs Value	-	1,026.97	-

Highest	Lowest
381.20	0.73
62.00	1.22
59.60	1.47
52.80	2.48
49.60	3.90

Stratify Command
(Numeric Fields)

Used For

To accumulate numeric information in a designated field for each stratum in a table or on a key field in a table that meets a certain condition.

When Used

Whenever the auditor wants to know the information about strata in a table as stated above. Auditors often stratify the same field repeatedly by using a different number of strata and strata criteria until the values in each stratum correspond to the auditor's needs.

Examples

- Stratify year-end accounts receivable into meaningful groups ($0 to $5,000; $5,001 to $10,000; $10,001 to $25,000, etc.).
- Stratify transactions by amount for a specific vendor.

TASK #1 — Stratify a Key Field in the Table

Steps

Because the Stratify Command requires you to enter a minimum and maximum value for the field you choose to stratify, first run the Statistics command on the key field before executing the Stratify command.

- *Click Analyze → Statistics. Running the Statistics command automatically generates and stores the minimum and maximum values for the key field so that you do not have to enter these values manually when running the Stratify command.*
- *Select the numeric or date field(s) you want to generate statistics on by clicking on the line(s) containing the field name(s). Use the Shift or Control key to select more than one field.*
- *Click OK.*
- *Close the Statistics command results portion of the window.*
- *Click Analyze → Stratify to open the Stratify command dialog. Each numeric field in the table is listed in the Stratify On drop-down list box. (See the top of the following page.)*

- Use the Stratify On drop-down arrow to choose the name of the field you want to stratify.

You must decide whether to accept the default setting for fixed intervals strata or decide your own intervals. The latter option is called Free. Free intervals allow you to customize the intervals you prefer, with or without equal intervals.

- If you want fixed intervals, decide whether to accept or change the minimum strata value, maximum strata value, and number of intervals. Change any or all of these if you choose.

- If you want a different number of intervals other than the default of ten, enter a new number in the Intervals box. If you want to suppress all items outside the minimum and maximum values, click the More tab, then click the Suppress Others check box. Otherwise, skip this step.

- If you want free intervals, click the Free radio button and enter the intervals you want in the box to the right. For each stratum except the lowest and highest strata, enter the end point of the stratum without commas or other notations. For the lowest and highest strata, enter the starting value each stratum. For example, entering 2000, 3000, 6000, and then 8000 provides the following strata: items less than $2,000, items between $2,000 and $2,999, items between $3,000 and $5,999, items between 6,000 and $8,000, and items over $8,000. See the illustration at the top of the following page.

▪▪▪ *Click OK to run the Stratify command.*

Command Results

The command results show information for each stratum: record count, percent of the total record count, total amount, and percent of the total amount. An example of Stratify command results is shown below.

As of: 02/16/2017 13:24:00
Command: STRATIFY ON Invoice_Amount FREE 2000,3000,6000,8000 TO SCREEN
Table: AP_Trans

Minimum encountered was 14.88
Maximum encountered was 56,767.20

Invoice_Amount	Count	Percent of Count	Percent of Field	Invoice_Amount
<2,000.00	75	73.53%	16.2%	45,128.15
2,000.00 - 2,999.99	9	8.82%	7.76%	21,625.25
3,000.00 - 5,999.99	7	6.86%	11.71%	32,615.51
6,000.00 - 8,000.00	4	3.92%	10.6%	29,548.42
>8,000.00	7	6.86%	53.73%	149,724.00
Totals	102	100%	100%	278,641.33

TASK #2 — Stratify a Key Field in a Table for Records that Meet a Certain Condition

The Stratify command can also be used with a filter to isolate certain records. An example is to run a conditional command to isolate all transaction amounts for a specific vendor. Do the following to run a conditional Stratify command:

 Complete all steps in Task #1 for Stratify, except do not Click OK to run the command.

 Click the If box.

Expression Builder - Stratify: If	

Expression

Verify

Save As

Available Fields

Name	Title	Start
Vendor_Number	Vendor_Number	66
Vendor_Name	Vendor_Name	74
Vendor_City	Vendor_City	120
Unit_Cost	Unit_Cost	145
Quantity	Quantity	58
Product_Number	Product_Num...	49
Invoice_Number	Invoice_Number	31
Invoice_Date	Invoice_Date	21
Invoice_Amount	Invoice_Amount	1

Buttons: `=` `<>` `And` `+` `-` `<` `>` `Or` `*` `/` `<=` `>=` `Not` `^` `()` `Date & Time...`

Filters

Variables

ABS1
AVERAGE1
COUNT1
HIGH1
LOW1

Functions

All

ABS(number)
AGE(date/datetime/string <,cutoff_date>)
ALLTRIM(string)
ASCII(character)
AT(occurence_num , search_for_string , withi
BETWEEN(value , min , max)
BIT(byte_location)
BLANKS(count)
BYTE(byte_location)
CDOW(date/datetime , length)
CHR(number)
CLEAN(string <,extra_invalid_characters>)
CMOY(date/datetime , length)
COS(radians)
CTOD(string/number <,format>)
CTODT(string/number <,format>)
CTOT(string/number)

☑ Paste Parameters

From Table

AP_Trans

`OK` `Cancel` `Help`

 Build the filter in the If box and click OK. See pages 6 through 9 for guidance.

 If you want to suppress all items outside the minimum and maximum values, click the Suppress Others check box. Otherwise, skip this step.

 Click OK to run the Stratify command with a condition.

Command Results

The command results show statistical information for the records that meet the specified condition. An example of command results for a conditional Stratify command is illustrated at the top of the following page.

As of:	02/16/2017 13:27:00
Command:	STRATIFY ON Invoice_Amount INTERVALS 10 IF Vendor_Number="11663" TO SCREEN
Table:	AP_Trans
Condition:	Vendor_Number="11663" (4 records matched)

Minimum encountered was 31.68
Maximum encountered was 4,870.83

Invoice_Amount	Count	Percent of Count	Percent of Field	Invoice_Amount
14.88 - 5,690.11	4	100%	100%	6,666.39
5,690.12 - 11,365.34	0	0%	0%	0.00
11,365.35 - 17,040.57	0	0%	0%	0.00
17,040.58 - 22,715.80	0	0%	0%	0.00
22,715.81 - 28,391.03	0	0%	0%	0.00
28,391.04 - 34,066.27	0	0%	0%	0.00
34,066.28 - 39,741.50	0	0%	0%	0.00
39,741.51 - 45,416.73	0	0%	0%	0.00
45,416.74 - 51,091.96	0	0%	0%	0.00
51,091.97 - 56,767.20	0	0%	0%	0.00
Totals	4	100%	100%	6,666.39

TASK #3 — Stratify All Records in a Table by a Character Field

The Stratify command can also be used with a filter to stratify certain records by classification. An example is to run a conditional command to stratify all transaction amounts in each of several districts. Do the following to run a conditional stratify command for each unique item in a character field.

Steps

 Before running the Stratify command in a table by a character field, you must first sort the table, by the character you select, into a new table. See page 81 for the Sort command. You will then do the Stratify command on the new table.

 Complete all steps in Task #1 for Stratify, except do not Click OK to run the command.

Click the More tab to open the More window. (See illustration that follows.)

- Click on the Break button to access the Selected Fields window.
- Select the field you want to classify by and make sure it is included in the Selected Fields box.
- Click OK to return to the Main command dialog.
- Click OK to run the Stratify command, organized by a character field.

Command Results

The command results show a separate stratification for each unique item in the character field you selected. (See the following illustration.)

As of: 02/16/2017 13:38:32

Command: STRATIFY ON Invoice_Amount SUBTOTAL Invoice_Amount FREE 2000,3000,6000,8000 KEY Vendor_Number TO SCREEN

Table: Sort_By_Vendor_Number

Vendor_Number: 10025

Invoice_Amount	Count	Percent of Count	Percent of Field	Invoice_Amount
<2,000.00	4	80%	4.35%	2,580.39
2,000.00 - 2,999.99	0	0%	0%	0.00
3,000.00 - 5,999.99	0	0%	0%	0.00
6,000.00 - 8,000.00	0	0%	0%	0.00
>8,000.00	1	20%	95.65%	56,767.20
Totals	5	100%	100%	59,347.59

Vendor_Number: 10101

Invoice_Amount	Count	Percent of Count	Percent of Field	Invoice_Amount
<2,000.00	3	100%	100%	691.04
2,000.00 - 2,999.99	0	0%	0%	0.00
3,000.00 - 5,999.99	0	0%	0%	0.00
6,000.00 - 8,000.00	0	0%	0%	0.00
Totals	3	100%	100%	691.04

Vendor_Number: 10134

Invoice_Amount	Count	Percent of Count	Percent of Field	Invoice_Amount
<2,000.00	4	80%	16.51%	3,735.28
2,000.00 - 2,999.99	0	0%	0%	0.00
3,000.00 - 5,999.99	0	0%	0%	0.00
6,000.00 - 8,000.00	0	0%	0%	0.00
>8,000.00	1	20%	83.49%	18,883.34

Summarize Command
(Character and Date Fields)

Used For

- To count and aggregate related records, accumulating numeric amounts for a character or date field.
- To count and aggregate related records for a combination of records using two character or date fields and a related numeric field.

When Used

When the auditor wants to accumulate information about each character in one field or two fields simultaneously, often to evaluate the possibility of unusual subtotals. Frequently used as an analytical procedure on every character field with three or fewer characters.

Classify, Summarize, and Cross-tabulate are all ways of accumulating information. The decision as to which one to use depends on the following:

- To accumulate percentages, use Classify.
- If data needs to be organized by a date field, use Summarize.
- If data needs to be organized by more than one character field simultaneously (e.g. by product number, by location), use Summarize or Cross-tabulate, depending on personal preference.

Examples

- Accumulate quantities of inventory by location for a table that includes a field for quantities on hand and a field for inventory location.
- Accumulate authorized pay per period for each job description by work department for an employee master file table.
- Accumulate daily sales by the date of the sale in a sales transactions table.

Steps

Click Analyze → Summarize to open the Summarize command dialog. Each character and date field in the table is listed in the Summarize On drop-down list box. (See the top of the following page.)

■■■ *Use the Summarize On drop-down arrow to select the character and/or date field(s) you want to summarize on. Use the Shift or Control key to select multiple fields.*

■■■ *In the Subtotal Fields portion of the window, click on the name(s) of the numeric field(s) you want to accumulate for each summary category. (See the top of the following page.)*

Unlike the Classify command, the Summarize command allows the user to include other fields in the summarized data. The other fields can be numeric, character, or date fields. ACL will include the contents of other fields selected for the first record that meets the unique combination of fields selected in the Summarize On portion of the command dialog.

In the Other Fields portion of the command dialog, click on the name(s) of the other field(s) you want to show for the first record in each summary category.

Click the Output tab.

By default, ACL sends the results of the Summarize to an ACL table unless you have already printed a Summarize command result to the screen or printer during the same ACL session.

- *To send the results to the screen, select the Screen radio button if not already selected.*
- *To send the results to a printer, select the Print radio button if not already selected. Then select Print in the Print window.*
- *To send the results to an ACL table, make sure the File radio button is selected and type a table name in the Name box.* Note: It is helpful to enter a meaningful name, such as Purchases_SUMM_ItemNo_Loc.
- *Click OK to complete the command.*

If the Summarize command results are saved to a table, the Summarize command creates a new table that contains the summarized data. Notice that there is a new table in the Overview window with the name of the new table you just created. In addition, the default view changes to the new summarized table.

Command Results

The command results show the following information:

- The number of records in each summary category.
- The total of the numeric field(s) selected in the Subtotal Fields box for each summary category.
- The contents of the numeric, date, or character field(s) chosen in the Other Fields portion of the window for the first record in each summary category.

An example of command results for a Summarize command follows.

As of: 02/16/2017 13:47:17
Command: SUMMARIZE ON WORK_DEPT_ SUBTOTAL GROSS_PAY OTHER WORK_DEPT_ EMPLOYEE_NUMBER TO SCREEN PRESORT
Table: Payroll

WORK_DEPT_	GROSS_PAY	Count	EMPLOYEE_NUMBER
«3 spaces»	0.00	1	«6 spaces»
A00	17,020.83	5	000010
B01	3,437.50	1	000020
C01	9,907.49	4	000030
D11	23,051.69	11	000060
D21	14,973.34	7	000070
E01	3,347.92	1	000050
E11	9,782.50	6	000280
E21	16,401.69	8	000100
E83	1,662.50	1	000320
Totals	99,585.46	45	

10 records produced

Σ Total Command

(Numeric Fields)

Used For

To total one or more data fields for the entire table or for records that meet a certain condition.

When Used

Should be used on every table when the table is first established. Numeric field totals should be compared to the IT department records or to accounting records being audited, when applicable.

Examples

- Determine totals for gross pay, deductions, and net pay columns in a June 30, 2018, payroll transactions table. Compare results to control totals received from the IT department.
- Determine total net pay on June 30, 2018, for employees in department #410.

TASK #1 — Total Numeric Field(s) in a Table

Steps

Σ *Click Analyze → Total to open the Total command dialog.*

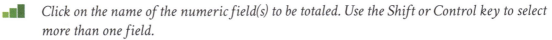

Click on the name of the numeric field(s) to be totaled. Use the Shift or Control key to select more than one field.

Click OK to run the command.

Command Results

The command results show the totals of all numeric fields selected. At least one of the control totals should be compared to documentation received from the IT department to verify the completeness and integrity of the table. Other columns may be compared with the client's financial totals, such as general ledger balances. An example of command results for the Total command follows:

As of:	02/16/2017 14:31:27
Command:	TOTAL FIELDS Quantity Invoice_Amount
Table:	Trans

Quantity	45,392
Invoice_Amount	300,682.04

Note: An alternate way to total a numeric field is to do the following:

- Click on the numeric field's column title so that the entire column is highlighted.
- Σ Click Analyze → Total Fields.

TASK # 2 — Total a Numeric Field in a Table Using a Condition

Steps

- Complete all steps in Task #1, except do not Click OK to run the command.
- Click the If button.
- Build the filter in the Expression box. See pages 6 through 9 for guidance.
- Click OK to run the command.

Command Results

The command results show the value of the numeric field(s) for records that meet the condition. The conditional Total command is useful in determining additional information about items in a population that meet certain criteria. An example of command results for a conditional Total command follows.

As of:	02/16/2017 14:33:47
Command:	TOTAL FIELDS Quantity Invoice_Amount IF Invoice_Amount > 5000
Table:	Trans
Condition:	Invoice_Amount > 5000 (17 records matched)

Quantity	7,474
Invoice_Amount	156,880.16

Verify Command
(Numeric, Character, and Date Fields)

Used For

- To check for data validity errors in a table, especially in numeric and date fields.
- To ensure that data in a table conforms to the table layout.

When Used

Should be used for every table when the table is first established.

Example

An auditor uses the Verify command after creating a sales invoice table from a client's data file. The Verify command isolates numeric, character, and date fields that are corrupted, such as an alphabet letter in a numeric field or a date such as March 32.

Steps

Click Data → Verify to open the Verify command dialog.

Name	Title	Start	Category	Length	D
Quantity	Quantity	20	N	8	0
Product_Number	Product_Num...	9	C	9	0
Product_Class	Product_Class	18	C	2	0
Invoice_Number	Invoice_Number	1	C	8	0
Invoice_Date	Invoice_Date	46	D	10	0
Invoice_Amount	Invoice_Amount	28	N	18	2

Verify dialog — tabs: Main, More, Output. Buttons: Verify Fields..., If..., OK, Cancel, Help

Click the Verify Fields button to open the Selected Fields window.

- Click the Add All button.
- Click OK.
- Click OK in the Verify command dialog.

Command Results

The command results show any records with invalid field data. Following is an illustration of Verify command results.

As of:	02/16/2017 14:37:27
Command:	VERIFY FIELDS Quantity Product_Number Product_Class Invoice_Number Invoice_Date Invoice_Amount ERRORLIMIT 10 TO SCREEN
Table:	Trans

0 data validity errors detected

** Notes **

Use this page to accumulate important notes.
